THE SETS ON VIETNAM

THE FIREBASE WAR

ROBERT B. HASEMAN

THE SUN SETS ON VIETNAM

THE FIREBASE WAR

ROBERT B. HASEMAN

ISBN: 978-1-4834-4585-4 (sc)
ISBN: 978-1-4834-4584-7 (e)

Because of the dynamic nature of the Internet, any web addresses or
links contained in this book may have changed since publication and
may no longer be valid. The views expressed in this work are solely those
of the author and do not necessarily reflect the views of the publisher,
and the publisher hereby disclaims any responsibility for them.

Any people depicted in stock imagery provided by Thinkstock are
models, and such images are being used for illustrative purposes only.
Certain stock imagery © Thinkstock.

Lulu Publishing Services rev. date: 2/24/2016

CONTENTS

For Dale Jackson and Phil Huth, KIA Vietnam
and Phillip Baucus, KIA Iraq

PREFACE

In 1969 when I led my platoon in Vietnam, the 3rd Marine Division was part of the III Marine Expeditionary Force. The 3rd Marine Division included three infantry regiments: the 3rd, the 4th, and the 9th. The division contained roughly 15,000 Marines, though less than a fifth of them were actually infantry troops. The other units in the division supported the infantry. The infantry regiments of 3rd Division contained about 4,500 Marines. Regiments included three infantry battalions each containing about 900 Marines. The battalions included three infantry companies composed of three platoons. The infantry troops did their jobs within these companies and platoons.

Infantry companies were usually commanded by a captain or first lieutenant, and platoons were commanded by new second lieutenants. The platoon I commanded contained about 35 Marines actually in the field. There were other Marines in my platoon who were injured or unable to serve, but they were in the rear area, not in the field. As a second lieutenant, I held the lowest officer rank but the highest rank in the platoon. The company commander was my boss. Second lieutenants ranked above all warrant officers and enlisted personnel. In the field, my platoon always included at least one sergeant, who was enlisted and usually of staff sergeant rank, to assist in command. The rest of my platoon was made up of corporals, lance corporals, pfc's (private first class), and privates. Each platoon was further subdivided into three squads of 10 to 12 Marines broken down into three fire teams consisting of 3 to 4 Marines. Corporals usually led squads, and lance corporals led fire teams.

There were nine ranks for enlisted personnel, five for warrant officers and 10 ranks for commissioned officers. Officers usually commanded units of enlisted personnel, or flew planes or helicopters. Warrant officers occupied the five ranks below commissioned officers but above the enlisted ranks. They often flew helicopters and had started out as enlisted Marines. I have arranged the ranks below, starting with the lowest private to the highest general.

Enlisted Ranks

Private E-1, Private First Class E-2, Lance Corporal E-3, Corporal E-4, Sergeant E-5, Staff Sergeant E-6, Gunnery Sergeant E-7, Master Sergeant or First Sergeant E-8, and Master Gunnery Sergeant, Sergeant Major, or Sergeant Major of the Marine Corps E-9.

Warrant Officer Ranks

Warrant Officer W-1 through W-5

Commissioned Officer Ranks

Second Lieutenant O-1, First Lieutenant O-2, Captain O-3, Major O-4, Lieutenant Colonel O-5, Colonel O-6, Brigadier General O-7, Major General O-8, Lieutenant General O-9, General O-10.

In war, military organizations are sometimes combined in inconsistent ways to complete a specific mission.

This discussion of organization and rank applies specifically to the Marine Corps. Other service branches use different titles for some of the ranks. For example, a Navy captain is of the same rank as a colonel in the Marine Corps. A Marine lance corporal is a private first class in the Army. The easiest way to compare ranks between service branches is to determine the "E" or "O" number, as in E-5 or O-8 and know that an E-3 in the Navy has the same rank as an E-3 in the Marine Corps.

HELLO VIETNAM

It surprised me to see the many fresh graves in the Vietnamese cemetery we passed by after leaving the rear area at Dong Ha. There were too many for a village as small as the one we'd just driven through. From our jeep, I looked at each Vietnamese peasant with suspicion, but as we drove west we lost contact with civilians and were alone as we bumped along the dirt road they called Route 9, headed toward our destination of Vandegrift Combat Base (VCB). It was my first day in Quang Tri Province, and I searched the terrain for signs of danger. I thought about the mine-clearing troops and wondered if they'd done a thorough examination on the road that morning. My driver didn't say much, but I'm sure he questioned why I hadn't just caught a ride on a helicopter; they flew back and forth all day. He

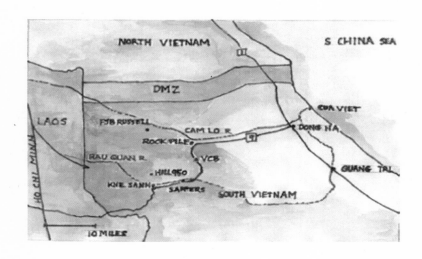

4ᵗʰ Marine Regiment area of operation

knew that unless he picked up a return passenger, and that was unlikely, he'd have to make the trip back alone. I guessed that my company's first sergeant thought his new platoon commander should get a ground view of part of the regiment's area of operation (AO).

When we arrived at VCB, I located my company at their assigned bunkers, which were spaced evenly along the perimeter of the base, and introduced myself to the commanding officer (CO), First Lieutenant John Matlock. Lima Company, my new unit, defended about a sixth of the perimeter, which was shaped as an oval and surrounded about 30 acres of low lying land just east of the mountains. The base had several landing areas, and a steady stream of helicopters transporting troops and supplies flew above. About 500 Marines manned the bunkers surrounding the combat base. Artillery, supply, and medical units performed their duties within the protection of the perimeter. VCB was the busiest base in the western half of Quang Tri Province and served as the supply hub for most of the activity in the area. To the west of VCB, mountainous jungle stretched into Laos and North and South Vietnam. This terrain provided concealment for our main enemy, the North Vietnamese Army (NVA), and they usually moved undeterred through the area. Whenever U.S. troops located NVA, we directed air and artillery strikes at their location, motivating them to stay hidden. Most of our firebases were placed strategically on high ground within this mountainous jungle. Mine-clearing activity on the portion of Route 9 that was west of VCB did not occur on a regular basis, so there was no vehicle traffic in that direction. Whenever we traveled west, transportation by helicopter was the only practical option.

On my first afternoon at VCB, we received enemy rocket fire, but the explosions weren't close enough to cause damage. I soon learned to use our heavily sandbagged bunkers whenever we heard the distant "pop" that signaled that rockets had been launched. The NVA would fire their rockets and rapidly leave their location because they knew we'd soon be aiming our artillery and mortar fire back at them. Receiving rocket fire in the afternoon from widely dispersed directions was a regular occurrence at VCB, but none of the Marines seemed very concerned.

As I write this memoir, I am 67 years old. Forty-six years have passed since I led a Marine infantry platoon in combat. Occasionally, over the years, I have told each of these war stories to my family and friends, but this is my first serious attempt to explain the entire experience. Accurate memories of the events in the stories remain clear in my mind. Most of the names of the individual Marines, our conversations, and some locations where activities occurred have faded from memory. As a result, in these stories I have fictionalized the names and conversations, but the characters they represented were real. In some instances, I combined events that occurred on separate patrols into a single story. I took all the photographs except the picture of Dale Jackson's gravestone. When the pictures were taken, I didn't record each location, so they're positioned in the stories based on my best recollection and may not have been taken for the story being told. Obviously, I wasn't always able to use my camera, so my watercolor sketches were added for illustration and mood.

In Vietnam, there was always a lot of personnel turnover within each company of Marines. The recent arrivals were called newbies, cherries, and FNGs (fucking new guys), and each of us served our time in that role. I had three different company commanders and three platoon sergeants during my six months leading a platoon, a fact that guaranteed a certain level of inexperience. Individual Marines came and went on a daily basis as their 13-month tours began or ended, or as they were wounded or killed. I didn't get to know anyone that well and really didn't try, since as an officer it was important to keep a little distance within the close confines of the platoon. Of the men with whom I served, I felt closest to my radio operator. He was always at my side with the radio available for my use, and we usually shared a bunker or poncho tent at night. He was also hardworking and loyal, and I liked him. I also have fond memories of the medical corpsmen in my platoon, and the other platoon and company commanders. As you might guess,

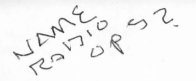

there were many unusual characters that remain in my memory.

I came to South Vietnam in March 1969, arriving by commercial jet that had disembarked from Okinawa, where we spent a night, before heading to Da Nang. I was assigned to my infantry unit: Lima Company, 3rd Battalion, 4th Marine Regiment, 3rd Marine Division, operating in Quang Tri Province, just south of the Demilitarized Zone (DMZ). As a second lieutenant, I was going to be a platoon commander for one of Lima Company's three active platoons, as soon as one of the other lieutenants left. Until then, I served as weapons platoon commander for a platoon without any assigned members, since the machine gunners and 60-millimeter mortar men who comprised that unit were attached to the other platoons. In combat, each of the infantry company's three active platoons, including the attached personnel, contained about 35 Marines. That was the approximate number in the field, but there were other members in the rear or in hospitals. In a peacetime environment the company included three regular and one weapons platoon, and each consisted of about 45 Marines. But the companies were never at full strength in the field.

New Marines came through what was called the battalion's rear area on the way to the "front." While the company's commanding officer (CO) was technically in command, the company's first sergeant was really in charge of anyone assigned to Lima Company's rear, which at that time was located in Dong Ha. In some ways it was a sorry place, because that's where the malingerers, deadbeats, and misfits from the combat companies were assigned. Some of these Marines had little respect for officers, their authority, or the mission. Drug use was prevalent in the rear but not at the front. In addition to the misfits and troublemakers, the rear area also included the battalion's legitimate rear area inhabitants, composed of the supply company, intelligence, operations, and medical personnel.

When we left the rear, we didn't say we were heading to the front, but rather the field, the bush, the boonies. Or we simply referred to the location where we were going, and everyone knew what that meant. A Marine's tour of duty lasted 13 months, but officers were assigned fewer days in the field than enlisted personnel. New infantry officers usually spent the first six months as platoon commanders and were then reassigned to battalion rear area responsibilities. The most accomplished officers later went back to the field to serve as a commanding officer or executive officer for an entire company of Marines.

We spent most of our time defending permanent combat bases, usually called firebases, located throughout the AO. These bases had names like The Rock Pile, Vandegrift Combat Base (VCB), Fire Support Base Russell, Fuller, and an assortment of smaller bases located on hilltops that were named for their elevation, like Hill 950. If we weren't assigned to these combat bases, we would be conducting field operations in the mountainous jungle between the spread-out firebases. We greatly preferred manning the permanent positions since they were well fortified and considered safer and more adequately provisioned. When we were on these bases, we conducted daily daytime patrols and night ambushes in the jungle outside of our base perimeter as part of our defensive strategy. In addition, we established several two-man listening posts (LPs) during the night in front of our fortified bunkers.

This was the beginning of the most dangerous and adrenaline-charged period of my life, where you could go from complete boredom to stress-filled anxiety in a second. We were all young, unfamiliar with the ruthless ways of war, and dependent on the judgment of our leaders. Due to the constant personnel turnover, many of us were inexperienced for a time, particularly the officers who spent less time in the field than the enlisted troops. I didn't doubt the intentions of our commanders; I'm confident that all tried their best. But I learned the importance of experience, competence, and luck in all the decisions that were made. Platoon commanders operated in a vacuum and were rarely given the "big picture," but nevertheless tried to do what was ordered. That really isn't much different from everyday life, but in combat the punishment for mistakes was deadly. A shroud of anxiety descended over me during that time, and I didn't recognize its weight until I felt it lift when I flew back to the "world."

CAN'T SWIM

Since I was not yet commanding an active platoon, my first assignment was to lead five Marines, borrowed from the active units, on a reconnaissance mission. My radio operator was a member of 2nd Platoon, and two Marines each from 1st and 3rd Platoons filled out the patrol. Our assignment was to set up an observation post about six kilometers from our base, which was located on the Cam Lo River. We set out after dark and soon reached the 100-yard-wide river, and walked along its bank moving upstream for about five kilometers. Then we left the waterway and climbed to the top of a nearby mountain. There, we concealed ourselves as best we could beside two rock outcroppings and began looking for signs of enemy activity. We had the option of calling in artillery fire or air strikes if we identified any enemy troops.

During our first two days on the mountaintop, we didn't see anything of interest. But just as the sun started to rise on the third morning, when I had the watch with the two Marines from 3rd Platoon, I spotted a small group of people moving across an open field on a nearby hill.

"Look, across the valley! Do you think they're NVA?" I whispered to the two Marines sitting next to me, Rodney Mobot, who was a private first class and Allen Fortney, a lance corporal. I took a quick look through my binoculars, then handed them to Fortney. I reached toward my radio operator, Corporal Tim Blitner, who was still sleeping alongside the two Marines from 1st Platoon after their late-night watch, and grabbed the radio, thinking I'd call the company commander (CO) about initiating an artillery strike on the suspected enemy patrol. We were operating in a "free fire zone," which meant we were authorized to shoot any person we encountered, and I knew that in Vietnam success was measured by confirmed kills.

Body Count /

"Hold on Lieutenant," Fortney responded as he leaned toward me, keeping his voice low and steady. "They're Montagnards and friendly, I'd guess."

The Montagnard tribesmen were a peaceful Vietnamese ethnic minority that lived in these mountains and were known to occasionally assist American troops. They weren't North Vietnamese Army (NVA) or Viet Cong (VC), as I'd suspected, but I was the new lieutenant and short on experience. I watched the calm demeanor of Fortney and Mobot and realized we were in no danger. The Montagnards never detected our presence and soon disappeared into the jungle.

After a few minutes, I turned toward Fortney and inquired, "How'd you and Mobot become such good friends?" Their names, it seemed, were always spoken together, but what made the friendship a little unusual was that Mobot was black and Fortney, white.

"Mobot and me played football together in high school. The Marine Corps had a buddy program where if you enlisted with someone you'd get to serve together later. Look what we got."

"Where'd you go to high school?" I asked, as Mobot lit his first morning cigarette.

"We went to Lawton High School, in Oklahoma, but we didn't finish. My girlfriend, Jannell, got pregnant, so I quit. Had to get a job, but didn't have much luck. Besides, I knew I'd get drafted, so I joined the Marine Corps with Fortney."

Then Fortney explained, "I shouldn't tell you this Lieutenant, but I was sentenced to the Corps. I got picked up for borrowing a car for a joyride and the judge gave me a choice: join up or go to jail. That's why I didn't finish high school." He pointed to the tattoo on his bicep with the letters U.S.M.C. "I was so happy to stay out of jail, I got this mark right after we'd finished boot camp, before I learned what a shit-hole place this is."

"What about you, Lieutenant?" Mobot asked. I could see that what he really wanted to know was how a smart white guy wasn't still at home with his college deferment. I gave him the short version of my story, but after I quit talking went back to my own thoughts and looked out on the mountainous jungle landscape in front of me.

I had plenty of time sitting on that hilltop to think about the "long version" of how I came to be leading a recon patrol in 1969 when I was 21 years old. In August 1967, after completing two successful years of college, I had enlisted in the Marine Corps while working at my summer job in Yellowstone National Park. I'd hitchhiked from Lake Village in the park to Butte, Montana, to sign up. Serving in the Vietnam War had been on my mind for over a year. Many of my high school friends were already fighting and dying in Vietnam, and I felt an obligation to participate. In 1967, if you were a young man and not in high school or college, you were very likely to be drafted into the U.S. Army. Some thought up clever ways to avoid service by claiming a medical deferment. Some escaped to Canada, but the vast majority of these sons of WWII veterans reluctantly accepted their fate and entered the armed forces. Enlisting while still having a college deferment was unusual, but I wanted to help, and for me helping meant fighting in combat, where I thought I could make the greatest contribution.

In Yellowstone Park I was employed by the National Park Service to fight a tree disease called white pine blister rust and, when needed, to battle forest fires that occasionally burned in the park. Our main job was to search the backcountry for a type of bush that was the intermediate host for the white pine disease, and then eradicate it with a tool called a hoe-dag and an application of herbicide. During the school year, I had been living with my parents in Columbia, Missouri, and attending the local university where my father and grandfather had been professors. Since I had enlisted in Montana, I was sent to boot camp in San Diego, where I graduated in the top seven of my class. That meant I was promoted to private first class, the second rung on the enlisted rank hierarchy. During boot camp we were tested for IQ, and my test scores were high enough to qualify me for Officer Candidate School (OCS), which would require a new three-year commitment if I decided to attend and was accepted. As a Marine junior officer, I would either fly a plane or helicopter or lead a unit of enlisted personnel.

I originally considered becoming an officer in the Marine Corps air wing, where I'd be a pilot and go through flight training after completing OCS. I learned that I'd need to pass the flight aptitude test before attending OCS and made the necessary arrangements, but subsequently failed the test. I took the exam immediately following a night of guard duty that had left me worn out, but perhaps I really didn't have the necessary aptitude. Since I couldn't become a pilot, I temporarily gave up my goal of becoming an officer and began Advanced Infantry Training at Camp Pendleton, California. There, I qualified for Scout Sniper School. Actually, I didn't really qualify, but my sergeant, who knew I was among the best shots during the rifle training, fudged my score. During the final qualifying test for marksmanship, my shots were in a tight group but I had incorrectly estimated the effect from the wind, so my shot–group was just out of the bulls–eye. The sergeant marked them in.

At Sniper School, I met the staff sergeant who convinced me to attend OCS and serve with the "real" Marines on the ground. His influence and encouragement led me to apply for OCS. "The Marines needed second lieutenants, and you'd be a good one" he said. At least I'd *be* one, and the sergeant was right; the Marines needed second lieutenants for Vietnam. College graduates weren't lining up in sufficient quantities to meet the demand. When the Marine Corps accepted me for OCS, they overlooked the requirement that an officer be at least five feet six inches tall. During the entrance physical I was instructed to leave my boots on when they measured my height, which provided me with the extra half inch needed.

In June 1968 I headed to Quantico, Virginia, to attend Platoon Leaders Class (PLC), which was what they called Officer Candidate School (OCS) when it was conducted in the summer. Some PLC candidates were still in college and needed to complete their senior year before returning after graduation to attend Marine Basic School. The rest of us headed to Basic School as soon as we finished PLC. At graduation, I remember our company's training officer wishing us well in Vietnam and then crying when he said goodbye. He was as hard-core as anyone but had just returned from

Vietnam before being assigned to PLC, and knew what we were in for.

I was sent to Quantico's Basic School class, TBS C 3-69, where we learned how to be officers and, to a lesser degree, gentlemen. Most of our time there was spent on tactics, leadership, and athletics, but we actually did have classes on place settings and proper eating technique. Upon graduation, I was selected to attend Army Ranger School for additional advanced training. Attending Ranger School with two other Marine officers from my Basic School class was an achievement, but it was made very clear to us that we were expected to succeed. "Marine officers don't fail Army training courses," the major said with emphasis. It was tough training, and only about half of those attending passed the course, but all three of us were successful.

Before being selected, I was asked to choose my military specialty as a reward for graduating near the top of my Basic School class. While infantry was the heart of the Corps and its largest component, there were other specialties like supply, artillery, and armor (tanks) that weren't considered quite as dangerous. My intention remained to serve in combat, so I chose infantry. Later when I was asked to choose between serving in two different areas in I Corps, I requested the area where I believed combat was most likely to occur because Marines in that sector had recently engaged in heavy fighting. Some might say my enthusiasm exceeded good sense.

As I reflected on past events, sitting on that mountaintop and looking out on the jungles of Quang Tri Province, I realized that my assigned AO was a beautiful place. I learned later that it was the Son Phan Cong National Forest Reserve. In America, this scenic place could be a national park. I felt lucky to have avoided serving in a populated area with civilians of unknown allegiance. In this western part of Quang Tri Province, everyone except our allies were considered enemies, and both our allies and our enemies were rarely seen.

After sunset on that third day of the recon patrol, we left our hilltop and proceeded down the mountain to the river, where we began constructing rafts using our ponchos. We wrapped the ponchos around wood and brush that we found along the riverbank. These poncho-rafts floated high in the water when they first entered the river. I could sense a little apprehension from Fortney and Mobot as they climbed aboard. We steered the rafts by quietly kicking our feet or using the butt stock of our M-16 rifles as paddles. It was my idea to use poncho rafts, influenced by my recent Ranger School training where I had learned how to make them. I admit that I was trying to impress with my "John Wayne cowboy" raft tactic, but it still seemed like a logical plan to me at the time.

We built three rafts with two of us on each one. My radio operator, Corporal Tim Blitner, was on my raft. Fortney and Mobot occupied another, and Fortney was equipped with an M-79 grenade launcher while Mobot carried an M-16 rifle. The two Marines from 1st Platoon, Moore and Hendrix, occupied the third raft and both carried M-16s. Once in the water, we tied the rafts together so we could quietly communicate with each other. As we floated down the Cam Lo River to rejoin the company, I evaluated my plan of conducting our return on rafts during the night.

Moonlight on the Cam Lo River

I noticed how the nearly full moon illuminated our position, and even though it was dark, we were still quite visible on the river. During training I had always welcomed moonlit nights, but on this night we wanted to remain concealed. I also realized we couldn't remain completely silent with our steering movements and scratchy radio transmissions. If we'd been spotted by Viet Cong or North Vietnamese Army soldiers standing on the bank, we would have made an easy target, and that thought left me feeling naked and vulnerable. I considered abandoning the float to walk along the riverbank, which would have been the better plan, but forged ahead, knowing that I hadn't properly evaluated all of my plan's shortcomings.

An hour later I realized the rafts were gradually sinking deeper into the river. Lance Cpl. Fortney announced, "Lieutenant, I can't swim, never learned." Instead of stealing cars he should have spent more time at the pool, I thought to myself, with a better understanding of his previous apprehension about getting on the raft.

While it would have been easy to leave the river, I realized that our rafts sinking into the water made us less visible, so we edged our rafts slightly to the shoreline and proceeded on. Fortney could probably stand up in the water anyway, I speculated. An hour later we were forced to leave the river when our rafts, which were still buoyant, had sunk about a foot underwater and we were wet up to our armpits and getting wetter. While the M-16s and grenade launcher "probably" still worked, Blitner informed us that the radio definitely did not. We had been regularly alerting our company of our progress along the river, but with the radio out of service, our communication with them ended. Our plan was to reenter our fortified position during the night. Now, without the ability to tell them that we were coming in, we were forced to spend the remainder of the night resting in the willow bushes growing beside the river.

As the sun rose, we disassembled our rafts to reclaim the ponchos and cautiously proceeded toward our firebase perimeter. With our radio still unable to transmit, Mobot yelled from safe cover, alerting the Marines manning the foxholes, "Don't shoot, recon patrol is coming in."

Although I was a little embarrassed about my corrupted raft plan, which resulted in our wet radio and disrupted communication, I didn't let it bother me for long. We had arrived safely. We were ready for a warm cup of coffee and a chance to let our clothes dry in the sunshine.

Looking back on this experience, I wish I'd accepted that the moonlit night made us vulnerable, and immediately left the river to walk along the riverbank. I was inexperienced and that would have been admitting that my plan was flawed, but it would have been the smarter move. This patrol was my first chance to lead and earn respect, and I had bonded with this small group of Marines. Although Blitner was the only one from that patrol to later serve in my platoon, I followed the progress of the other four Marines as we served together with Lima Company.

ANXIOUS THOUGHTS

It wasn't a week after returning from the reconnaissance mission that Lt. Lewis, the 2nd Platoon commander, was wounded in the foot while leading a daytime minesweeping patrol along Route 9. He was medevac'd out, and I assumed command of the 2nd Platoon. As the commander, I reunited with Corporal Blitner, who became my constant companion serving as my radio operator. Whenever I needed to talk to anyone, he was always nearby to dial up the radio frequency and hand me the transmitter. Several weeks later Lt. Lewis returned from the hospital hoping to reclaim 2nd Platoon. I objected because I was getting to know the personnel, knew they were good, and didn't want to go through the process again with a different platoon. The captain decided Lewis and I should flip a coin for the platoon. I won, and Lewis was assigned to 3rd Platoon, which had recently become available after the former commander rotated to the rear.

During the time Lt. Lewis was injured, 2nd Platoon was ordered to Hill 950, in western Quang Tri Province, to operate independently from the rest of the company. This was not unusual; on several occasions during my six months in combat, platoons would be separated from their company to conduct independent action. The position we were assigned to defend served as a place of observation on top of a steep 950-meter hill. It had a good view of the abandoned Khe Sanh Combat Base, which was located on the valley floor, and we could see the old airfield inside its perimeter. Our position was about four kilometers north of Khe Sanh and 20 kilometers south of the DMZ. The former combat base was located on the Rao Quan River and was also adjacent to Route 9, which continued west into Laos. The old combat base was originally constructed in August 1962 by U.S. Special Forces and was used to monitor NVA infiltration originating from the nearby Ho Chi Minh Trail.

There were hundreds of small trails that veered off the Ho Chi Minh Trail in Laos and moved through the Rao Quan Valley and around the many steep hills surrounding Khe Sanh Combat Base. In 1959, construction of the Ho Chi Minh Trail began after Ho announced his revolution to reunify all of Vietnam, and the trail became the main supply route for the NVA. It started in North Vietnam and coursed through Laos and Cambodia before reentering Vietnam and ending near Saigon. Throughout the war the Americans bombed much of the trail, attempting to interfere with the NVA's delivery of supplies. The bombing was controversial since the United States wasn't officially at war with either Laos or Cambodia. Of course, Ho had planned the route so much of the trail would be outside of Vietnam, hoping to avoid its destruction by North Vietnam's enemies. Between April 29 and July 22, 1970, Americans and the Army of South Vietnam (ARVN) sent ground troops into Cambodia, but the effort to disrupt the movement of supplies along the trail was only temporary.

Most of the hills surrounding Khe Sanh were named for their elevation, such as Hills 881N and 881S, and Hills 861, 558, 950, and 1015. Many battles had been fought for these hills between April 1967 and July 1968, because control of the high ground was necessary for the protection of the combat base located on the valley floor. Between January and July 1968, as many as 40,000 NVA soldiers had attempted to defeat the Marines at Khe Sanh, and the siege became one of the most famous battles of the war. Descriptions of the fighting dominated the news, and some reports were comparing the siege to Dien Bien Phu, which was the location of the final French defeat during the first Indochina War in 1954. In reference to Khe Sanh, President Johnson is thought to have declared to his war council in February 1968, "I don't want no damn Dien Bien Phu," meaning he didn't want Khe Sanh to be our final defeat.

The fighting at Khe Sanh intensified in January 1968, about the same time as the NVA Tet Offensive began. The Americans were surrounded and constantly bombarded by NVA artillery, rockets, and mortars fired from high ground controlled by the NVA. Resupply by air became the only way to keep the base provisioned, but bad weather delayed some of the flights. The turning point came in July when the Americans reestablished use of Route 9 so resupply could then also come by truck. Throughout the six-month siege, American air strikes took a tremendous toll on the massed forces of NVA, which precipitated their withdrawal in July 1968. After the NVA retreated, the United States came to the conclusion that the presence of the combat base did not prevent NVA infiltration through the thick jungles and wasn't worth the necessary military commitment to keep it open. Khe Sanh was closed by the Marines within a month, and shortly after, the NVA declared the abandonment of the base as a victory. However, Hill 950 continued as a place of observation and the only permanent Marine outpost in that area of high NVA activity.

We'd all heard the stories about the dangerous area surrounding Hill 950 and worried about the NVA presence. Nearly every night, illuminated tracer rounds, spaced evenly between the regular machine gun bullets, could be seen flying across the valley floor. An ARVN battalion was conducting a jungle operation south of the Rao Quan River. The battle for Khe Sanh had ended ten months before, and now that the base was abandoned, the NVA had little difficulty moving through the area. The ARVN operation was a short-term attempt to disrupt the NVA movement.

Our hilltop, which had a good view of the airstrip, was defended with nine fortified bunkers and the well-sandbagged command post where I spent my night watch. A helipad was located at the center of the perimeter and another was just outside the wire. A wrecked Chinook-47, shot down in some previous hot landing, lay sideways on the hill a hundred meters below our perimeter. It appeared that the old chopper had been used for target practice, and it had large gaping holes on each side of its body.

The vegetation surrounding the hilltop had been partially removed by a defoliant, probably Agent Orange. Razor-edged concertina wire encircled the perimeter, radiating out in front of the lines in waves. Access trails wormed through the wire. Piles of C-Rations stood between the

Command post at Hill 950

sandbagged bunkers and the pungent latrines, which were made from half of a 55-gallon steel drum and placed on either side of the helicopter landing pad. The distinctive odor from the adjacent "piss tubes," which were PVC pipes extending into the ground, embellished the smell.

After a Marine finished eating a can of C-Rats, he would toss it outside the perimeter of bunkers to join the thousands of cans already lying there. The cans needed to be put somewhere, and the thinking was that they would rattle if the enemy attempted to infiltrate our position. They also rattled most every night from the wind and from rats eating the rotted food they still contained. This tinny noise always created anxious thoughts. Anxious thoughts weren't mind-numbing fear, but rather a mixture of fear-inspired anxiety and imagination. This type of anxiety was always close to our consciousness in Vietnam.

It wasn't hard at all to imagine that NVA sappers might probe our position, and when the cans rattled, that fear came to life. The sapper units were composed of highly motivated, suicidal NVA warriors who would attempt during darkness to crawl naked through the concertina wire to reach the foxholes. Since they didn't wear clothes, there wouldn't be anything to catch on the wire. They carried satchel charge bombs, which could be thrown at our bunkers. Once they breached a perimeter, they would engage in hand-to-hand combat with the Marines and often be reinforced by regular NVA infantry that followed behind. Their effectiveness and dedication to their cause could be compared to kamikaze pilots and suicide bombers; we had great respect for their courage and feared their abilities.

To protect our position from sapper attacks, we established listening posts (LPs) in front of each perimeter. These LPs consisted of two-man teams carrying a radio, and we would typically establish two or three LPs in front of each defensive position. The unlucky Marines who drew the assignment did not usually dig foxholes; they were expected to return to the safety of the perimeter if they heard an approaching enemy. The flaw in this concept is easy to see. If the LPs returned to the firebase because of a falsely perceived attack, they might be thought of as wusses, and no Marine wanted that label. But if they waited until they were certain and initiated defensive gunfire, they knew they'd have difficulty distinguishing themselves from the enemy when they attempted to reenter the perimeter. This nighttime duty was a dangerous assignment, and some thought the LPs only served as sacrificial lambs for any approaching sapper. The duty was necessary for the overall safety of the unit, but the Marines selected as LPs cursed their bad luck.

Our perimeter was oval shaped, with the machine gunners carefully positioned so their fire could cover the ground in front of all the nearby foxholes and crisscross with the fire from the other machine guns. The 60-millimeter mortars were placed near the command post so their fire could be directed to all sides of the base. The riflemen, with their M–16 fully automatic rifles, occupied the remaining bunkers, and each Marine knew the direction he would fire if the command "Fire the Final Protective Line" (usually stated as "FPL") was given. The Marines also knew where the LPs were located so our fire would avoid hitting their location. When the command was given, it would initiate fire that was low to the ground and intended to cover an area about 30 meters in front of the perimeter to protect the position during an enemy assault.

In Ranger School, I was taught that firing the FPL at several prearranged times each night also served to keep the troops awake, alert, and well-practiced in the tactic in preparation for an actual firefight. It seemed to me that firing the FPL also served to discourage sappers from sneaking up to our bunkers, since their approach would take hours and they couldn't know when we might initiate our low to the ground rifle fire. We never randomly fired the FPL when we were on an operation in the jungle since we intended to conceal our location. However, when we were defending a permanent position, our location was already well known, and resupply choppers kept us well provisioned with ammunition. We didn't need to worry about running out. I was always surprised that Marine training did not emphasize the random firing of the FPL as a routine nighttime defensive tactic. I found that I was one of very few platoon commanders who employed it and attribute that tactic to preventing sapper attacks on my platoon. In spite of its use, however, we still had anxious thoughts every night and especially at Hill 950.

Each of the nine bunkers was assigned two or three Marines who would alternate being on watch. My command post included my radio operator, Blitner, Platoon Sgt. Washington, his radio operator, and our platoon's corpsman, Doc Roller. Blitner was from Wyoming and had joined the Corps after flunking out of college in 1967. Washington, who was on his second tour in Vietnam and hailed from Alabama, planned to make the service his career. Roller, who also had attended college, was from Texas, and while he was technically a Navy Hospitalman Third Class, he always conducted himself like a dedicated Marine. About 70 percent of the platoon came from poor rural backgrounds, with Caucasians in the minority and Black and Hispanic Marines representing the majority ethnic groups.

Fog engulfed our position on the second night after arriving at Hill 950. I heard an unexpected single rifle shot fired from the Khe Sanh side of the perimeter followed by an ongoing volley of fire from the rest of our bunkers. The deep thuds originating from the M-60 machine guns and the explosive crack from grenades echoed through the darkness and haze that surrounded our hilltop. As I left the command post with Sgt. Washington, I heard Blitner yell out, "Lieutenant, watch out when you approach the bunkers, the fog will make them jumpy." I'd always wondered how I'd perform when the bullets started flying, and figured I'd soon find out.

As I left the command post (CP), I nodded at Blitner to thank him for the advice, then Washington went one way and I went the other. We couldn't see 10 feet in front of us. I announced my approach through the darkness as I came to each bunker. "Lieutenant coming in; where are they, which way is the fire coming from?" The Marines answered with short responses as they kept their focus in front of them, firing while they spoke. I worked my way around the perimeter and learned that someone had been shot. It seemed obvious that we were under attack. Most of my platoon had never experienced a firefight before; the tension was high, but everyone seemed in control.

As I reached the valley side of the perimeter facing Khe Sanh, I approached a bunker where a fallen Marine lay on his back. I heard an experienced squad leader scream at another trooper, "What really happened Velasquez? That wasn't gook fire. That wasn't an AK–47; it was an M–16. You shot Chico, didn't you?"

Velasquez collapsed to his knees and began to shudder and cry.

"I didn't mean to . . . my rifle just fired." He explained how he was carrying a can of C–Rats in one hand and his rifle in the other, holding it near the end of the barrel. The rifle slipped from his hand with the butt end hitting the ground. The safety was off because they thought, as Velasquez said, "Charlie was close. I didn't mean to shoot my friend. I'm sorry Chico, I'm sorry."

As I realized the true situation, Sgt. Washington yelled out, "Cease fire! Cease fire!" The gunfire gradually subsided, and then it was deadly quiet.

Chico lay on his back with a puddle of blood and brain tissue forming around his head. It was such a small, neat, round hole on his forehead. How could that have done it? When I extended my fingers under his head, I felt a fist-sized hole where the bullet had exited and immediately pulled my blood-wet hand back, wiping it on my pant leg. This was my first experience with a dying Marine—heck, I'd never seen any man die. I realized that Doc Roller's compressions on Chico's chest would do no good. He still quivered but Chico was gone.

Blitner brought me the radio and I called the company commander and ordered a medevac. About 30 minutes later, we heard the lonely sound of distant helicopter rotor blades as they approached our position. A Huey medevac, with its lights shining through the foggy darkness and its blades making that distinctive "wop, wop, wop" sound, found its way to our landing pad. Chico's limp body was carried on board. Velasquez followed behind him, head down, still whimpering.

We couldn't help but feel sorry for Velasquez. He and Chico had been best friends. They had served together for most of their 13-month tours and eagerly anticipated their return to the "world," where they planned to customize a car together. How could he have shot his best friend in the head? They would now return home a few weeks earlier than expected, but I don't think Velasquez would ever view his return as a happy occasion. He'd broken the rules by taking his rifle off safe with a chambered round. You didn't do that until you needed to shoot. Certainly not while preparing food at your foxhole on a quiet, angst–filled night. But I suspected that safeties were often disengaged when anxious thoughts filled a young Marine's head. I began to realize that human error was a big part of combat and war; I was becoming less naïve.

A report came in to us later in the night that Chico had arrived at the field hospital but Velasquez couldn't be accounted for. We wondered if he'd jumped out of the Huey on its way back to Quang Tri. As morning light reached our hilltop, and after the LPs had rejoined the platoon, we learned that Velasquez had arrived safely but snuck away while the attention was focused on Chico. I never learned if Velasquez faced a court martial or if Chico's parents ever learned that their son died from "friendly fire."

Helipad on Hill 950

View toward Khe Sanh airstrip

MEDEVAC

Before we left Hill 950, and a few weeks after Chico was killed, I led a reinforced squad on a daytime patrol into the valley of the Rao Quan River near the abandoned Khe Sanh Combat Base. It was warmer than usual that morning as we began the patrol, and I could tell it was going to be a very hot day.

After moving through the concertina wire that surrounded our hilltop, we were especially alert as we descended into the jungle that concealed the enemy. We moved carefully in a line with our best point man out front, everyone looking for danger. Perspiration soon made our utilities wet, and the jungle sounds kept us vigilant. After a few hours the point thought he'd spotted an NVA soldier hiding in a concealed bunker about 100 meters in front. I realized that this could be my first *actual* firefight, and I carefully considered what we should do. We were too close to call for an air strike unless we backed away, and since we hadn't received any enemy fire, I ordered the Marines carrying M-79 grenade launchers to lob a few of their little bombs at the bunker, and then the machine gunners to open up with a rapid blast of bullets, neither of which elicited any enemy response. I ordered the squad into a frontal assault formation and, feeling a bit uncertain, advanced on the bunker with our rifles pointed forward. We didn't fire any more shots since none were fired at us, and when we reached the bunker, the NVA soldier was gone. There was no blood or any evidence that we'd hit anyone, so we continued on our patrol.

About half an hour later we reached the Rao Quan River north of the Khe Sanh Combat Base and could see the remains of the airfield, buildings, and bunkers within the old perimeter. The base had only been abandoned for 10 months, but new vegetation was already enveloping the ruins. We formed a defensive circle, placed LPs out in front, then sat down and took a break to eat our C-Rats for lunch.

"Corporal, do you think an NVA soldier had been in that bunker?" I asked Blitner.

"I heard Williams say he saw him there too. He said the gook must have di-di'd (left in haste) as soon as he spotted us."

Blitner's confirmation made me more confident that we had actually confronted an NVA soldier, and I changed the subject. "What made you decide on being a radio operator, Tim?"

"After I left college I figured I'd be drafted, so I enlisted in the Corps. My recruiter suggested I go through Communication and Electronics School where I'd learn a skill."

I thought to myself but didn't say it aloud: He didn't tell you that you'd be a prime target carrying that radio with its long antenna, you and the lieutenant (myself) standing nearby, holding the transmitter. But I hadn't thought of that either.

What I did say was, "Tim, I'm glad you're with me. How many more days do you have here?"

"Just 127 days and a wakeup; I can't wait to get back to Wyoming. It's quiet there." All the Marines kept track and knew exactly when they were scheduled to leave.

"What are you going to do when you get back?" I asked.

"Probably try to get back in college, if they let me. If I can't get in, I'll try something in electronics at Vo-tech."

In the early afternoon we reloaded our packs and arranged our gear to begin the long climb back up the mountain to our 950-meter hilltop. The return seemed to be going smoothly, but we were sweating heavily and suffering from the 115-degree heat. I intentionally slowed our pace, taking many breaks as we climbed. Suddenly, word was passed up the line that a Marine was down, apparently suffering from heatstroke. When I moved back to his position in the line, he lay barely conscious, attended by the corpsman.

I remembered that during OCS, the summer heat in Quantico, Virginia, was so intense that all of our daytime hikes were accompanied by large trucks carrying tubs of ice. If a Marine suffered heatstroke and needed to be cooled, the tubs of ice would be available. In the OCS class before mine, an officer candidate had died from heatstroke.

The trucks carrying tubs of ice became a standard measure after that.

There were no streams nearby to cool our heatstroked Marine, so I immediately called for a medevac. Before the helicopter reached our location, Sgt. Washington advised me that three more Marines had succumbed to what looked like the same malady and lay beside the game trail we'd been following. We could hear the CH-47 medevac as it approached and threw red smoke grenades to mark our location. The helicopter soon hovered above our position. Ropes, with gurneys attached, were lowered through the jungle canopy so we could load our comatose Marines, one at a time, up into the medevac. I couldn't help but worry as the chopper flew back to the field hospital where the Marines would be cooled down.

Our patrol continued the strenuous ascent, and we reached the top of Hill 950 an hour later, worn out from the heat and exertion. I thought about the long day and our near miss at combat with the NVA soldier in his bunker. In later years I sometimes wondered if the NVA ever used the same tactic as Sioux warriors had in the 1866 Fetterman

Massacre. There, a small group of Indians made a hasty retreat hoping to decoy the cavalry that followed closely behind into an ambush by the rest of the war party.

The next morning the four Marines returned to rejoin their squads. Had any of them faked their affliction to get helicoptered out, I'll never know, but they convinced me.

MOVIES ON THE BEACH

After leaving Hill 950, we relocated to Cua Viet Beach, a location we looked forward to defending. Cua Viet Beach was east of Dong Ha, along Vietnam's South China Sea, and was considered to be an in-country rest and recuperation (R&R) base. Our company was part of a battalion of infantry assigned to occupy the foxholes surrounding the base. The bunkers were positioned around the perimeter and even along the beach, to protect against an enemy assault. The east coast of Quang Tri Province was heavily populated compared to the mountainous western part where most of our activity was concentrated. The western side of Quang Tri Province was designated a "free fire zone," meaning that Marines were authorized to shoot any person we encountered. The area on the eastern side of

Quang Tri Province, which included Cua Viet Beach, had many civilians, so of course this area had different rules of engagement.

Our new location was considered much safer than Hill 950, but it was still a dangerous place. We had confronted the NVA in the central and western part of Quang Tri Province, but at Cua Viet the threat came from Viet Cong (VC). The VC, dressed as civilians, blended in with the general population and only attacked Americans when they held an advantage, which wasn't often and mostly at night. The VC were known to set booby traps, a threat we hadn't previously encountered except when Lt. Lewis was injured by a small booby trap that day on Route 9.

We had more free time at Cua Viet, which allowed us the opportunity for a swim in the ocean and time to enjoy the service clubs on base. Every night a movie was shown. An outdoor screen had been constructed on the beach, and we would sit in the sand and watch the movie, listening to the audio through speakers located on either side of the viewing area. Hot showers were available at Cua Viet Beach, and food was cooked in a mess hall.

We even had cold beer, and thought the base was heaven.

We still, however, had to take our turn defending the lines. It wasn't every day, like at other bases in our AO, but every other day we positioned two or three Marines in each foxhole in our assigned sector. I manned a command post with Sgt. Washington and our radio operators, and we would take turns on watch, checking in with our riflemen, LPs, and higher command. The troops assigned to each bunker were supposed to alternate resting and being alert—three hours on, three off. Once each night, Washington or I would walk the lines checking on each position to ensure the posted guard was awake. But at Cua Viet, it soon became apparent the Marines were much more relaxed, and sometimes when we approached a foxhole we found everyone asleep.

"Wake up Marine, keep your eyes open, there are VC out there, and they want to cut your throat." I'd yell out. While sleeping on guard duty was a court martial offense, it wasn't widely enforced at Cua Viet Beach, or anywhere else, for that matter.

If it had been enforced, we could have lost 10 percent of our troops to court martial, and we needed them all. My punishment was to assign the miscreant to "shit burning duty" the next day. Our latrines were mostly 55-gallon drums cut in half, and when they filled every few days, it was necessary to burn them by pouring kerosene in the drum and setting it on fire. You can get an idea of how that smelled by imagining burning shit and kerosene mixed together.

At Cua Viet we also conducted daytime patrols in the surrounding savanna, and sometimes came upon Vietnamese vendors carrying boxes of Cokes and snacks that were for sale for a dime or in exchange for several cans of C-Rats. "You want Coca-Cola Marine? Hershey Bar?" some Vietnamese hawker would ask, as if we were at some sporting event back home. It was hard to stay focused when vendors were in the area.

Could we trust these guys? I know I didn't. When we set up a temporary resting position and created a defensive circle, we'd usually position LPs out in front. Once I discovered that I was getting volunteers to serve at the LP; that was so unusual it made me suspicious. What could be going on outside our perimeter that was so enticing that volunteers were lining up to serve? "Some mama san and her daughter are selling it out there, Lieutenant," Washington advised after checking things out. We immediately pulled the LPs and continued our patrol.

One day on patrol, we found a table next to the road with boxes filled with propaganda leaflets. The messages emphasized that blacks in Vietnam were dying in far greater numbers than whites and that they were being "put up front" in Vietnam. The leaflets didn't seem to faze any of the black Marines in my platoon. I couldn't really know for sure—and no one would tell me—but it was apparent to everyone that blacks outnumbered Caucasians in the infantry, and that's where most of the deaths occurred.

We returned from patrol anticipating the movie we'd enjoy on the beach that night. We relaxed in the sand, beers in hand, and watched John Wayne in the World War II movie *The Sands of Iwo Jima*. During the movie, just as mortar explosions appeared on the screen, we heard a pop nearby

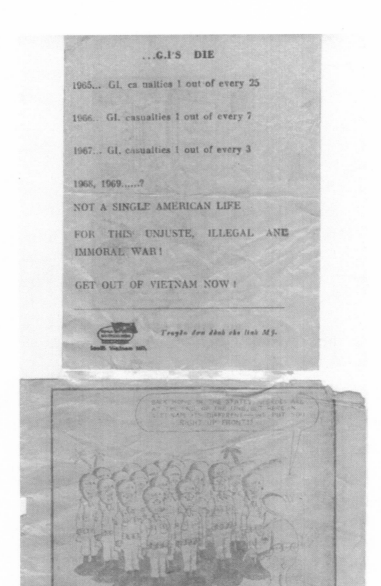

Propaganda leaflets

that was decidedly more realistic. Someone yelled, "Incoming!" We rushed to our bomb shelter bunkers located alongside the viewing area just before the explosions hit the beach. Rocket fire was a regular occurrence at Cua Viet Beach, and had injured Marines in the past, but this time the bunkers prevented any injury. The timing with the movie seemed surreal; was it a VC joke? Did the sloppiness created from our perception of safety make Cua Viet Beach a more dangerous place than Hill 950? Probably not, but every rocket fired had the capability to kill.

NIGHT AMBUSH

In July 1969, the 4th Marine Regiment, which included my battalion, conducted an operation in the mountains and jungles just south of the DMZ on the western side of Quang Tri Province, north of Khe Sanh. The battalion commander coordinated the movement of our unit with the other two battalions of the regiment. Our mission was to "search and destroy" as we moved east across a 35-mile stretch of jungle. My company was never close enough to the other companies to see or hear them, but our commanders knew the location of every other unit. The platoons of Lima Company were also separated most days and operated independently, but would come together at night when we would be resupplied with ammo and C-Rations and receive the mail. Sometimes I'd receive letters from Sharon, a girl who had dated my friend Dale Jackson in high school, before he was killed in Vietnam.

Occasionally, the choppers would bring in warm beer, which we'd drink in the evening after the foxholes were dug. In Vietnam, servicemen were allocated two beers a day, but because of logistics or maybe greedy supply personnel, it never worked out that way for the Marines in the field. We went without beer most days, but when it did arrive we'd have five or six cans and get a little drunk. We certainly weren't going to throw the beer out or carry it in our packs; they were heavy enough. Warm beer never tasted so good.

When we moved as a platoon, we were usually in a long line that started with the point squad of about 10 Marines. I trailed behind them along with Blitner and Doc Roller. The middle squad was behind us, followed by the platoon sergeant and his radio operator, who usually traveled with the 3rd squad.

Navigating a platoon through a densely canopied jungle using a topographic map was not easy because the canopy blocked the view of nearby high ground, making it difficult to locate our unit's

Chinook–47 delivering supplies

position. But it was my responsibility to read the map, plot the correct direction, and convey the orders to the point squad in order to arrive at our desired destination.

Every squad would take its turn at point. The point squad leader would choose one Marine to act as the point man for the platoon. The point had the responsibility to protect the platoon by using his observational skills and alertness to detect danger and avoid ambushes and booby traps. Usually only the best Marines from each squad were put on point, and even though the position was dangerous, certain Marines sought it out and took pride in being selected. I remember one Marine on his second tour who had been busted in rank once or twice but was a real stud at point. He would move confidently through what was often heavy vegetation, and the platoon felt more at ease when he was out front.

We operated in high temperatures that routinely exceeded 110 degrees Fahrenheit, and regularly endured heavy rain, especially during the rainy season. Our camouflage utility uniforms were worn without underwear, and we avoided using socks. Our boots, which were made from a camouflage canvas-like material, had eyeholes to drain water, so wearing socks only delayed drying. Whenever we walked through streams or wet areas, we'd check ourselves for leeches. The uniforms would get sweaty and dirty within hours of being washed, and the resupply helicopters provided us with replacements every week when the ones we wore were too filthy to bear or wash ourselves.

In addition to the oppressive heat, the weight of what we carried made hiking difficult. Most Marines carried their M-16 rifle and 15 to 20 extra magazines, each holding 20 rounds of ammunition. Each man had four to six grenades attached to their steel-reinforced flak jackets and aluminum-framed backpack. We worried about the pins on the grenades staying in place, and we checked them regularly. Some Marines carried Claymore mines, used for ambushes and protecting defensive positions. The machine gunners had their heavy weapon and carried bands of ammunition. The mortar men had their M-16s and either the steel mortar tube itself or the mortar stand, both of which were heavy. They also packed extra mortar shells.

The radio men had their radios in addition to the other gear they carried. The backpacks were filled with cans of C-Rations and usually held a poncho and poncho liner, which was a light quilted blanket that would dry out in minutes after getting wet. It was very cold at times on those mountaintops, and we needed our liners. We all wore steel helmets, carried several canteens of water and a large K-Bar (Bowie) knife, and referred to ourselves as "grunts" for obvious reasons.

With all the weight from the gear and food we carried, and the ever-present daytime heat, it didn't take long to tire. Especially when we had to use our K-Bar knives to cut vegetation so we could move forward. As the point and platoon tired, it became easier to cut corners and miss signs of trouble ahead. We might follow a well-defined trail that could be booby-trapped rather than continue slogging through heavy vegetation. Exhaustion lowered motivation for staying alert—and even our determination for staying alive. It interfered with cogent decisions, and at times, death seemed almost like relief from fatigue.

After arriving at our night positions, I would meet with the company commander and the other platoon commanders to discuss company plans. We were fortunate to have First Lt. John Matlock as our company commander (CO.) He'd been a platoon commander during the first part of his tour and then was assigned as Lima Company's CO during his final months; he knew what he was doing.

After consulting with the CO, I conducted my own meeting with 2nd Platoon's three squad leaders and the platoon sergeant to decide assignments for the night. If my platoon had been chosen for the night ambush, I'd pick a squad for that mission and designate which squads would provide Marines for the LPs. We arranged check-in times and determined exact locations for each duty. Then foxholes were dug, including the one for my command post. Marines wrote letters home and treated jungle rot infections with antiseptic. Doc Roller spent much of his time on our everyday cuts, because they festered in the heat with the dirt and sweat constantly entering the wound. Sometimes they looked like they'd never heal. Ponchos were made into tents whenever we expected rain. Blitner usually constructed the shelter, when we built one, and also dug the foxhole I shared with him. Most nights we slept without shelter on the ground next to our foxhole, and if it rained we got wet.

One night, after my platoon was selected to conduct the night ambush, I chose to lead it with a squad of 8 Marines. Lieutenants usually didn't lead night ambushes since the entire platoon was his responsibility, but I felt a need to show that I could. Blitner, of course, was at my side with the radio. We planned to set up the ambush along a trail that we thought was used regularly by the NVA. In the daytime we tried to avoid trails; at night we used them because they were easier to follow and much quieter than tramping through the brush and grass in the dark. We knew the NVA used the trails at night for the same reason. It was said that the Americans owned the day and the NVA and VC owned the night, because if it was too dark for us to see the enemy, we couldn't take advantage of our superior fire power. I know most of us feared the night much more than the day, especially on dark moonless nights like this

Dark mood on night ambush

one. At around 11:00 P.M., we quietly set up our position about 20 feet to the side and parallel to the trail. Each Marine was positioned so he was close enough to touch the Marines on each side and hear whispered instructions passed down the line. I was in the middle. Each of us tried to position ourselves behind a tree trunk or a log or some indentation in the ground, but we could never completely shield ourselves like we could with a deep foxhole. We placed Claymore mines between our location and the trail. Claymores were concave-shaped explosives, shaped that way so the embedded shrapnel would explode only in the direction the mine was aimed. We would hold the firing mechanism in our hands, and it would be activated after enemy troops moved into the kill zone.

Everyone tried to remain as quiet as possible. Still, someone would clear his throat or make a muffled cough, and the radio, turned to its lowest volume, would make a scratchy static sound as we clicked the transmitter at prearranged times to let the company know we were OK. When you're sitting in an ambush, you notice exotic sounds coming from insects and animals of the jungle, and each one is evaluated to determine if it could be an approaching enemy. The crescent moon gave off very little light but still enough to see an enemy soldier moving cautiously down the trail. Each Marine alternated guard duty with someone else, but none of us slept very much. Those anxious thoughts came with a vengeance. Would we see a single NVA soldier or would there be two, or would it be an entire squad or maybe a platoon? How long could we wait to decide the strength of our enemy before we'd start firing? Just a few NVA would be easy to kill, but if their numbers were overwhelming, would we simply hold our breath and let them pass by, only 20 feet in front of us?

It was my call, and I knew I'd have difficulty assessing enemy strength. Would I be able to see far enough in the dim moonlight to estimate the number of NVA moving down the trail? Did I even want the ambush to happen? To open fire on an armed but surprised enemy would validate our mission. We were in Vietnam to kill them, weren't we? But if a large group moved into our kill zone, we weren't likely to get them all before they returned fire, and fighting with only 20 feet of separation using automatic rifles was a scary thought. I admit that I hoped there wouldn't be a firefight, but I would have pulled the trigger that night. I'm glad it wasn't necessary. When morning light arrived, we picked up our gear, repacked the Claymores, and headed back to our company position.

"Next time, Lieutenant," Blitner observed, with irony.

CONFIRMED KILLS

Crazy things happened on jungle operations. Heck, crazy things happened everywhere in Vietnam. One afternoon, my company took fire from a machine gun located across a valley a mile away. Its tracer rounds, coated with phosphorous, were spaced evenly between the regular rounds and showed us the trajectory of the bullets and where the enemy gun was positioned. Earlier that day, we had encountered what we thought were NVA soldiers, but didn't get any shots because the enemy quickly moved out of the area. We pursued them for a few hundred meters but gave up when it seemed they had evaded us. Perhaps the machine gun fire came from that same group of NVA troops.

What did we do? Like every infantryman in Vietnam in a similar situation, we called in air

Airstrikes on NVA machine gun position

strikes and artillery fire. Within 10 minutes, several fighter jets were dropping their explosives, and artillery rounds found our target. It was quite a display and must have cost the U.S. government plenty.

It was fun to watch—that would teach the NVA to shoot at us. After dropping their bombs, the jets soon left the area. As they disappeared over the horizon, the NVA opened up with that machine gun again, not expecting to hit us because we were too far apart, but rather letting us know that they were still there. They were telling us they'd won that fight; "bring it on," they seemed to say.

Once, while on patrol, I motioned for a corporal carrying an M-79 grenade launcher to come forward. I pointed to where I wanted his grenade to land, on what could have been a bunker, about 50 meters away. He fired, but the grenade nicked a hanging branch about 10 feet ahead and exploded. A small piece of shrapnel from the exploded grenade embedded into the corporal's forehead. As we all belatedly hit the ground, we heard the corporal scream, "It burns! It fucking burns."

At least he was screaming expletives and wasn't dead. The shrapnel had only gone in skin deep; it hadn't penetrated the skull. Doc Roller treated the wound as best he could with his limited medical kit, and after it cooled off we continued the patrol. The corporal had to endure the embarrassment of having a piece of metal hanging from his forehead until Doc removed it later that day.

During the jungle operation, we saw several monkeys and, once while resting in camp, a short green snake, probably some kind of viper. Someone said it was a "five stepper." If it bit you, you'd be dead before taking five steps. The wildlife was just part of the parklike environment we operated in. We killed the snake and a few of those monkeys. I still feel bad about the monkeys.

Have you ever really seen it rain? I'm talking four inches in an hour rain. We had rain like that one night while on the jungle op. We set up in a drizzle, but then the rain really started coming down hard for several hours. Our foxholes filled with water, and even though we were all soaking wet we didn't want to get down in them. It would have been like sitting in a puddle. Who knows,

Lt. Haseman, hamming it up

maybe the leeches would have found us in that water. After dark on that rainy night, we positioned our LPs out in front as usual. One LP team didn't go to the position they were assigned, but rather stayed far too close to our perimeter. During the night someone thought they heard enemy movement nearby and launched an M-79 grenade in the direction of the sound. The LPs frantically radioed in and told us to quit firing; it was landing near their position. Later they admitted that they hadn't gone out far enough.

While the jungle was thick with unknown green vegetation and the dampness and humidity kept us uncomfortable, we had very few biting insects to contend with; just the leeches, and they weren't insects. I thought we'd be bothered by mosquitoes, but fortunately they never caused us serious problems after an application of bug repellent. Once, I broke out with blisters on my arms and face and thought I'd touched poison ivy. Doc gave me a shot that quickly cured my problem and diagnosed the malady as hives.

Toward the end of the month-long operation, I led my platoon through the jungle on our way to a rendezvous point where we planned to meet the rest of the company. While walking along the sidehill of a mountain, we came upon a trail that was much wider and more heavily used than others we had seen. We decided to follow it through the jungle canopy. I split the platoon so half of the Marines were in a line on each side of the trail. Soon we entered an area where the main trail was perpendicularly intercepted by well-spaced smaller trails that defined an area used as a camp. Each cross trail was about 50 meters on either side of the main trail. Tree branches had been made into frames for tents, and in places, tables had been constructed that looked like they'd been used as operating tables for a hospital. Bunkers had been built around the perimeter of the area, but none of these fortifications and structures could be seen from the air, which made them much less vulnerable. We listened for sounds of danger.

The camp could have held a company of NVA, probably more. Sgt. Washington found me and whispered, "Near those hospital tables are grave-like holes and some are filled with fresh dirt. I think bodies are buried there. Some are empty, probably ready for someone dying on the table." We dug up the closed graves to confirm they contained bodies. Later, 2nd Platoon received "credit" for each dead soldier, my platoon's only confirmed kills. In Vietnam, estimates of dead enemy were not allowed; we only counted those confirmed as being dead. As we continued to inspect the camp, we found fresh NVA "tire sandal tracks" on the ground and some discarded trash, but the enemy was gone, we were pretty sure.

In one of the uncovered graves, we found several artillery shells. They looked like misfires that were being saved for use in booby traps. You could see where the firing pin had made an indentation on the end of each round. Blitner contacted the captain's radioman, and I asked the CO what he wanted us to do with the shells. "Should we leave them or bring them back with us so our demolition experts can blow them up?" The CO instructed us to bring them back, so I assigned several Marines to carry them and we headed out. Our line was unusually well spaced, especially on either side of the Marines carrying the artillery shells. As we moved along, I wondered how big a hole the explosion of a shell would make and how far the shrapnel would fly? What had caused the misfire? Were the shells stable? The captain and I could only guess at the answers, and once again we relied on fate, as we did nearly every day in Vietnam.

"Keep your space Marine," Sgt. Washington instructed.

We worried about the artillery shells exploding for another three kilometers, but we reached the company safely and, as planned, detonated the shells. Unfortunately, the explosion started a brush fire, which marked our location and burned several acres before we gave up trying to control it and moved away to find a different night position. Thinking back, I believe it would have been smarter to have buried the shells in a concealed location that the NVA would never have found. If a shell had exploded and killed Marines, that mistake would have haunted me forever. I should have simply buried the shells before advising the CO. Sometimes, wrong decisions made by leaders had deadly consequences. Was it Napoleon who said he'd rather have lucky commanders than good ones?

FIREBASE

We spent a lot of time defending the widespread hilltop firebases in the mountainous jungles of Quang Tri Province. Each firebase served as the defensive infrastructure for launching daily patrols and night ambushes to discourage the enemy from moving into and through our regiment's area of operation (AO). The task of preventing enemy incursion was difficult if not impossible due to our inability to detect the enemy's presence as they passed through the jungle. The strategy required most of the regiment's troops just to occupy the firebases. It discouraged, but failed to prevent, the NVA from passing through the jungle on their way south or from attacking our firebases, so long as they maintained their will to fight, which they did. This defensive strategy was much less effective as the more traditional "attack strategy" that is usually employed in war.

Sunsets on firebase

Our daily routine was to conduct squad-sized patrols in the jungles surrounding the firebases. The patrols were usually led by a squad leader, but once a week either Washington or I would lead the mission, and when that happened we would typically increase the size of the patrol. Each evening we'd plan the night ambushes and choose the locations for the LPs. We posted Marines in each of our bunkers during daylight hours, but after the sun set we became much more alert to sounds outside the perimeter. The danger to our firebase mainly came at night, so when we weren't on guard or patrol, we had plenty of time to take care of routine personal duties.

The ever-present dust and sweat made our utilities filthy as soon as we put them on. Using my helmet as a washbasin, I tried to wash my clothes and body at least every other day. When on a firebase, we shaved regularly and had time to tend to our festering jungle rot sores. We also had plenty of time to bullshit with other Marines, clean our M-16s, write letters home, and think up ways to improve the taste of our C-Rats.

We'd go to great lengths to improve the taste and always tried to prepare C-Rations in our own special way. The usual solution was to add cheese, included in the box, and special spices, usually obtained from care packages sent from home. Popular condiments were Tabasco and soy sauce, dried onion soup mix, and garlic salt. Most of us had settled on our favorite meal and ate the same concoction almost every time. My favorite was beans and franks that I doctored up with cheese and Tabasco. Other meal choices included turkey loaf, beefsteak, ham and limas, chopped ham and eggs, boned chicken, and spaghetti and meatballs. The boxes also included one can of apricots, pears, peaches, or fruit cocktail. Each box might include pound cake or crackers and had a small pack of cigarettes, jam, and cheese spread, along with one of the military's great inventions, the P-38 can opener. It worked great on the cans and, when folded, was about the size of a small rectangular Band-Aid.

The C-Rat choices might sound pretty good, but they all had a similar unpleasant flavor, probably as a result of preservatives or the suspected mystery ingredient we identified as saltpeter, intended to reduce libido. The cans were all dated, so you could see when they were packaged. I remember some being left over from World War II, making them 24 years old in 1969. There were plenty of crates of C-Rations located on each firebase, so finding a favorite meal was never a problem; you'd just have to sort through the boxes until you found the right one. Stacks of unpopular food choices lay off to one side of the crates, and rats scurried between the boxes.

There was always time to strike up a conversation on slow afternoons. Once, during an officer's meeting, the conversation turned to OCS, and I had the chance to tell the others my story about an officer candidate named Bill Hastings, who was a bit of a screw-up.

Military schools always arranged their participants in alphabetical order, so at OCS, Bill and I lined up next to each other in every formation and soon became friends. Toward the end of the course, we were going through a series of inspections that would partially determine our ranking in class. One of the inspections was of each candidate along with his military duffle bag filled with his personal belongings. We spent hours spit-shining our boots and preparing our uniforms so they would be properly creased. Our personal items were arranged in our duffle bags as required by guidelines in the Marine Corps Handbook. We shaved carefully and attempted to avoid cutting ourselves. At the scheduled time, our company was called into formation with each of the three platoons aligned next to the others. Bill and I took our place on the end of the third row of the 2nd Platoon. We were ordered to remain at "parade rest" until such time as the inspecting officer was directly in front of us, then we would come to attention during the inspection. The inspecting officer started with the front row of 1st Platoon, about 50 feet from our location.

I glanced at Bill and noticed that he had forgotten to shave that morning. He was always behind in his preparation and must have overlooked this important task. I whispered to Bill, informing him of his mistake, and watched out of the corner of my eye as he began to align himself by using the position of other Marines as a shield to conceal his movement from the inspecting officer. Fortunately, the inspector was concentrating on the Marine located directly in front of him. Bill opened his duffle, reached to the bottom and, after a minute of searching, pulled his razor slowly from the bag. He started to dry shave, moving carefully to avoid detection. He had to feel his face with his fingers to ensure he didn't leave any stubble. His results were about what you'd expect: He cut himself twice and missed cutting whiskers in a few spots. As the inspecting officer moved in front of our platoon, Bill carefully placed the razor back into his duffle and repaired the alignment of his uniform, readying himself for the inspection.

The inspecting officer finished with me and stood in front of Bill. Bill came to attention, looking straight ahead as he knew he should. The inspector looked him over and, as you'd predict, castigated Bill's shaving ability, pointing out the missed spots of stubble and the blood clots on his face. That set the tone for Bill's inspection; he was failing long before the officer opened his duffle and found the razor on top, out of place in the bag. Bill failed the inspection but I think he still eventually passed OCS (PLC).

Bill was on the two-course plan at OCS, still attending college, so he returned for his senior year when most of us moved on to Basic School. I would guess that he graduated OCS near the bottom of the class, since he was always getting demerits for some mistake. In spite of that, he probably became a decent Marine officer. He was never intimidated, fearless, and very likable. Nearly all the junior Marine officers I served with were competent and physically athletic, and I was always proud to be associated with them. I never learned how Bill fared in Vietnam, but I suspect he survived; he was adaptable.

One afternoon on a firebase, Blitner informed me, "The CO's radio operator just told me we'd be receiving a visit tomorrow morning from our regimental commander." What could he want? I thought to myself. During my six months in combat, we had only one visit from regimental brass. The next day the commander and his staff arrived by helicopter around 9:00 A.M.

Clouds below firebase

They soon set up folding tables and began cooking a hot breakfast—real food, including bacon, eggs, and hash browns. When we finished breakfast, some of the regimental Marines brought out drums and electric guitars and began playing rock music with amps. This was as close as we ever got to a real USO show. I wondered what the NVA were thinking as the loud music ricocheted off the hills. They played for an hour while the regimental staff cleaned up the tables and packed up the food.

The officers had a short meeting with the regimental commander before he flew back to the rear. He gave us his speech about winning the war and leading our troops. "And one more thing," the colonel said and began pointing out what he described as discrepancies with our hilltop firebase. "There are too many big rocks inside the perimeter, your walkways needed to be better defined by arranging those rocks alongside each trail, and the base needed to be tidied up." It should be made to look more like the regimental rear area, I thought to myself. As the choppers departed from our position, I organized a work party to make the "improvements" the colonel had suggested, and yes, there was a little grumbling. It hadn't been a high priority to keep the firebase that neat, and I suspected it would take more than tidy firebases to win this war.

Fortney and Mobot on LP

SHORT TIMERS

We were all "short timers." We knew it in early summer 1969 when we heard on Armed Forces Radio that President Nixon had announced the withdrawal of the 3rd Marine Division. At that time we didn't know which regiment of the three comprising the division would go first or the exact date we'd be leaving, but we knew we were "outta here" and heading back to the "world." The announcement may have made us a bit complacent and lowered our guard, like a horse galloping eagerly and less aware back to the barn after a long ride.

In early August 1969, my company was separated into three platoon positions. The company commander, with 1st Platoon, was in a fortified permanent position above a corner on Route 9 between VCB (Vandegrift Combat Base) and Khe Sanh. Their position on a low hill was likely established to provide security at a crucial place on Route 9 and had clear fields of fire on all sides of the perimeter.

About 1,500 meters to the east, 3rd Platoon was ordered to establish a new position overlooking Route 9 on another low hill. Their new location had jungle to the north but was clear of jungle to the south so they could see along the road. When they established the new position, they had to dig foxholes and make other defensive decisions related to the terrain. Their perimeter was essentially like the positions we established each night while on jungle operations, except on jungle operations we moved every day. In this case, 3rd Platoon would remain on their new perimeter for a week or more, giving the enemy more time to assess their opportunities for attacking the position. However, Lima Company had not been attacked once since I arrived, so no one seemed worried.

My platoon was ordered to occupy a permanent firebase located on a steep hill in mountainous jungle terrain three kilometers to the south. My position was well fortified and controlled a very

defensible hilltop, but it was intended to be occupied by a larger force than just one platoon. The
3rd Marine Division consisted of three regiments,
the 3rd, 4th, and 9th, and by early August the 9th
Regiment had already been withdrawn, leaving
our expanded regimental AO undermanned.
There were too many bunkers on the firebase for
my platoon to cover, so some were left unoccupied.

We had been there for only a few days when the
sappers attacked 3rd Platoon's recently constructed
position on Route 9. Because the position was only
recently established, their defenses were the weakest
of the three platoons. Their foxholes weren't as
deep, and they didn't have sandbags or concertina
wire providing additional protection. On the day
of the attack, two LP teams had been positioned in
front of the perimeter around 10:00 P.M., placed in
separate locations in the jungle about 100 meters to
the north. One of them was occupied by Rodney
Mobot and Allen Fortney, two of my former recon
patrol Marines. I can only imagine how they spent
the last two hours of their lives.

"What was that?" Mobot whispered.

"Shut up Bot; night noises, that's all." Fortney answered back.

"I need a smoke!" Mobot said.

"Not now, LPs can't smoke. You know that."

"Why'd we get LP again? We just had it last week." Mobot complained.

"We got it because we got it. Look, I'll sleep first. Wake me in two hours." Before Fortney leaned back on the damp ground, he clicked the radio transmitter button two times, making the 11 o'clock check-in. Fortney knew that attacks usually came between 2:00 and 4:00 A.M. and wanted to be awake then.

Mobot looked out below a jungle canopy that allowed very little light from the fading moon to reach the ground. He thought about home.

I wonder what Jannell is doin' tonight. She better be doin' what she promised.

A few minutes later, he heard a suspicious sound again, causing more anxious thoughts.

That ain't no monkey. Should I wake Fortney? He just thinks I'm hearing shit. Hell with it! The hell with him. I need a smoke. If I hold my helmet near my chest and light it underneath, no one will see the light. Fuck it! There now, that's better, he thought as he exhaled the smoke.

Fifteen minutes later, Mobot heard a sound that was very close. "What's that? Oh God . . . Jannell . . ." were Mobot's final words, and then he exhaled for the last time.

"What the f . . ." Fortney gasped as he began to sit up, before the knife entered his chest.

It was after midnight when the LPs quit reporting to the platoon command post. The hand-to-hand combat started soon after that, when the sappers entered 3rd Platoon's perimeter.

The CO quickly determined that my hilltop location was too far away to reinforce 3rd Platoon, but we were best situated to establish a communication link between 3rd Platoon and the battalion operation officer, who was located in Dong Ha. The battalion radios were unable to communicate directly with 3rd Platoon because a nearby mountain interfered with radio transmission. I began my communication by talking with Lt. Lewis's radio operator, Lance Corporal Gary Howard.

"Can I speak to the actual?" I asked, hoping to speak to Lt. Lewis.

"The lieutenant can't talk now, too much shit going on." The radio operator responded.

"How many are there? Are they inside your lines?" I asked.

The radio operator didn't answer right away, but when he did he said, "I . . . I've been shot through my thigh . . . give me . . . a minute." When he responded he said, "About 15 sappers, I think, it's hard to tell, everyone's fighting, bayonets, knives . . . too close to fire."

Soon, the transmitter from our second radio was handed to me, with the major from S-3 (the battalion's operation department) on the other end. "What's going on with 3rd Platoon, lieutenant?"

I told him the situation as Howard had described. "Can you bring gunships; they're inside the lines?" I screamed into the transmitter.

"Repeat it again, how many NVA are there, where are they located?" The major asked.

"I told you already, 15 sappers inside the lines . . . What can you do? They're dying down there sir." I was speaking with too much emotion, not with the calmer demeanor I should have maintained.

I reached for the other radio transmitter connected to Howard and 3rd Platoon, telling him that "gunships are coming." Again, he didn't answer right away; I think he'd passed out. But I heard desperate shouts and screams in the background, made by Marines and NVA fighting for their lives.

A minute later I heard Howard's voice, which was weak and unsteady as he answered "need help." The noise from gunfire and exploding grenades interrupted his words, making them hard to understand.

Several gunships with Gatling gun capability soon hovered over 3rd Platoon's position. These were the rapid-fire gunships we sometimes called "Spooky," which were only employed in dire situations. Battalion couldn't use the Douglas AC-47 fixed-wing planes we called "Puff" (named for a popular song) because the planes weren't capable of getting close enough so the gunners could distinguish between individual NVA soldiers and the Marines fighting hand to hand inside the perimeter. Planes dropped illumination flares that lit up the area. It seemed like daylight over the overrun perimeter.

The company commander radioed that he was sending a squad of reinforcements from 1st Platoon. They left their perimeter and headed down Route 9 toward 3rd Platoon's position. The reinforcement squad soon came under fire from NVA located in the jungle on the hillside north of Route 9. It was obvious that the sappers inside 3rd Platoon's foxholes weren't acting alone. A few minutes after the rescue squad was attacked, 1st Platoon's undermanned perimeter began receiving fire. Sappers often worked in conjunction with NVA infantry, and it was apparent that there were more than 100 enemy troops in the area, far more than just the number of sappers attacking 3rd Platoon.

The battle raged at both 3rd and 1st Platoon's locations and along Route 9. The NVA never breached 1st Platoon's perimeter, but the gunfire and explosions in front of their lines indicated the intensity of the fight. The Spooky gunships with their rapid-firing guns hovered over both 1st and 3rd Platoon's positions, attempting to pick out enemy troops while avoiding individual Marines. The heavy fire from the gunships lasted for about 30 minutes, tapering off first at 3rd Platoon's position but continuing at 1ˢᵗ Platoon's hilltop. When the firing subsided, most of the sappers were dead, although some may have rejoined the surviving NVA infantry soldiers as they disappeared into the jungle.

The four Marines from the 1ˢᵗ Platoon rescue squad that weren't wounded or killed finally reached 3ʳᵈ Platoon's overrun position after the attack had ended. They began helping the wounded and loading the dead Marines into the arriving medevacs.

3ʳᵈ Platoon suffered 12 KIA (killed in action), four of whom had been on LP duty. The LP Marines had all died from knife wounds without firing a shot. They may have fallen asleep but more likely were just overpowered by the sappers. The other eight Marines died fighting hand to hand inside the perimeter. Nearly everyone else in 3ʳᵈ Platoon had been wounded, with very few Marines still fit for duty. Those few huddled silently in shock. Lt. Lewis, earning his second Purple Heart Medal, and the platoon sergeant were both wounded and evacuated. One of the squad leaders was now in charge of what was left of the platoon.

The rescue squad from 1ˢᵗ Platoon had two KIA and four wounded Marines. Among the Marines who remained on 1ˢᵗ Platoon's hill, four were KIA and 18 were wounded. They found 17 NVA dead inside 3ʳᵈ Platoon's perimeter, but there must have been others who were carried off by surviving enemy soldiers. The enemy's dead and wounded at 1ˢᵗ Platoon's location were removed by their compatriots, so we couldn't determine their numbers.

I've estimated the number of KIA and wounded for each platoon with help from a book edited by John S. Bowman, titled *The Vietnam War: An Almanac.* There, in the chronology, I found the entry from the official records describing this August 10, 1969, battle. It reported: "Ground War; North Vietnamese soldiers attack two U.S. Marine bases 1500 meters apart near the DMZ. The attackers, using grenades and dynamite bombs, kill 17 Marines and wound 83. Seventeen enemy bodies are found inside the perimeter of one Marine camp."

The number of wounded reported in the *Almanac* may be high, because it exceeded the number of Lima Company Marines who were actually in the fight. My platoon defended the mountaintop firebase three kilometers to the south, leaving approximately 70 Marines from 1st and 3rd platoons defending the two outposts that were attacked. The report indicated there were 83 wounded and may have included additional Marine casualties inside the hovering gunships or possibly other Marines from the battalion inserted into the perimeters during the fight.

The battle filled me with emotion. It first appeared when I heard the desperation in the radio operator's voice and the screams in the background, and later when the CO reported and we remembered our dead. Mobot and Fortney were good Marines, and so were the others. I recalled how I'd won the right to keep 2nd Platoon in that coin toss with Lt. Lewis back in April. 3rd Platoon would have been my command if I'd lost that toss. It seemed a long time ago when I decided to join the Marines with the intention and desire to help my country by fighting in combat.

Didn't the NVA know we were short timers? We would have been withdrawn soon anyway. We were young and strong and at our best. We had lives to live back in the world, and girls to meet and enjoy. We had families to build and careers ahead of us. For those of us that survived, we had a new appreciation for life. I'm still haunted by the memory of that night. It was my company's only firefight, and my role was simply to man a radio on a nearby hill, safely away from the shooting. But I *was* there with 3rd Platoon—at least I was emotionally. The 1st and 3rd Platoons did the actual fighting while the "lucky 2nd" defended its remote mountaintop, but I was there.

In many ways I wish I actually could have been with 3rd Platoon. In the same way that I sought to join my countrymen in Vietnam, I wanted to fight alongside my company's 3rd and 1st Platoons. I joined the Marines with a desire to help my country's cause in combat. But after that battle, I was relieved to have avoided the consequences. It's a conflict in my mind. Hand-to-hand combat is something I wish I could say I survived because it would have validated my imagined intentions. Whenever I tell this story, the emotion returns. Those dead Marines have always deserved that feeling; it's the least I could give them.

EXPLODING FIRE SUPPORT BASE RUSSELL

Fire Support Base (FSB) Russell was located in western Quang Tri Province, on a hilltop along a ridge east of Laos and south of the DMZ. The perimeter was shaped like an oval and was about two acres in size. On one end of the position, a battery of 105mm howitzers (cannon-like guns) was set up to provide fire support for Marine activity in the area. Several times every day and night, loud repercussion from the artillery broke the silence on the hill when the guns fired in the direction of a target identified by some Marine unit in the field. Bunkers were spaced evenly around and inside the perimeter, and it was defended by a company of Marine infantry. Concertina wire encircled the defoliated hill below the fortifications, and the base looked similar to the other hilltop positions in western Quang Tri Province.

Fire Support Base Russell

Lima Company was ordered to occupy FSB Russell while the base was going through the process of being closed and destroyed. The base had been built only a year before, but with President Nixon's announcement of the withdrawal of the 3rd Marine Division in the summer of 1969, many hilltop bases were being abandoned. Some bases were turned over to the South Vietnamese ARVN forces, but others, like Russell, were blown up.

One morning, after we'd been at the base for a week, Blitner informed me, "The CO's radio operator just heard a report from battalion that two Marine positions had been attacked by sappers last night."

It sounded similar to the sapper attack that we had suffered the month before, with two positions in close proximity being hit simultaneously. The attacks were against a company in the 3rd Regiment while it was conducting a jungle operation near FSB Russell, the same general location where 4th Regiment and our battalion had conducted an operation in August. We had heard the howitzers firing their rounds the previous night, which must have been in support of those Marines.

John S. Bowman's book, *The Vietnam War: An Almanac*, again has the entry for that September 17, 1969, sapper attack. It stated: "Ground War; North Vietnamese troops assault two US Marine outposts just below the DMZ, killing 23 Americans and wounding 24. In one attack, several communist soldiers manage to breach the camp perimeter of the Third Regiment of the 3rd Marine Division. The attacks are finally repelled by artillery and air strikes. A total of 23 North Vietnamese are reported killed in the two attacks."

Those two battles, the one involving my company on August 10, and the one against the 3rd Regiment Marines on September 17, 1969, were the only two sapper attacks reported in the *Almanac* for Quang Tri Province during the six months I served there in combat. However, just before I arrived in Vietnam, on February 25, 1969, Fire Support Base Russell, and another base called Fire Support Base Neville, located 10 kilometers to the west, had come under simultaneous attack by two large units of sappers and infantry. Neville was attacked first, followed by the attack on Russell. Sappers breached both bases, and the battles resulted in 43 American deaths. As described by Captain Albert H. Hill, who was there during the attack, "Fire Support Base Russell also came under attack, obviously in an effort to destroy the guns located there. Once again, the attack began with a heavy mortar barrage, and supporting artillery fire from within the DMZ. Sappers from the 27th NVA Regiment quickly breached the northeast perimeter of the base. In the first few minutes, the 81mm mortar section and the company CP, both located on the east and southeast side were decimated." Those three 1969 sapper attacks were similar in that each one was conducted against two of our positions at the same time. The most recent attack just reminded us once again that the NVA were willing and able to attack our well-fortified positions.

The following week, large helicopters came to FSB Russell to remove the artillery in preparation for the demolition of the base. A day later, on September 21, 1969, we watched the engineers begin the destruction of the base by placing explosives inside each bunker in a daisy chain, so called because each parcel of explosives was attached to a detonation cord running to the adjacent bunkers. At the appropriate time, the explosion would be initiated and each position destroyed, one after the other, until the circle of explosives played out.

The captain ordered my platoon to board the first CH-53 helicopter that landed. The CH-53 was the largest helicopter used to transport Marines, and it was big enough to hold an entire platoon. Later we'd meet up with the rest of the company at FSB Fuller on Dong Ha Mountain. Each of the other two platoons planned to board additional CH-53s that circled above the base, leaving the engineers to blow up the hill.

After we lifted away from the firebase, I was talking on the radio with the CO's radio operator, who suddenly informed me that the hill had exploded prematurely, and Cpt. Clingman, our CO, had been wounded in the head and buttocks. I could hear several explosions on the radio as we flew away. Cpt. Clingman had replaced Lt. Matlock when he rotated out in July. The captain, also a competent officer, had the habit of wearing his rank insignia on his cover (hat). That wasn't the safest practice in combat because; the rank insignia could reflect sunlight and attract enemy snipers. I respected him and hoped his injury wasn't too bad.

In a 1969 letter to my parents, explaining the FSB Russell incident, I wrote: "Anyway, that accident I was talking about; my platoon was airlifted out just before the firebase was accidentally exploded. It was pretty bad even though only about 1/3 of the demolition went off. We lost some people and had countless minor injuries. We were lucky . . . very lucky that some of the troops pulled some of the detonation cord out of the TNT before they blew. The strange part was that at the time we had with us on the base a couple of Kit Carson scouts (former NVA) that we could not find anywhere. They were the only people we couldn't account for; so we left without them." I'd always suspected that those former NVA scouts had detonated the explosives and then escaped into the jungle. If they had blown up in the explosion, we should have found some of their remains.

Much later I would learn that there was one other person who couldn't be accounted for . . . ever be accounted for. I didn't learn about Lance Corporal Jimmy Jackson until around 1993, when

I received a call from Ron Martz, a writer for the *Atlanta Journal-Constitution*, and at that time, author of two books about Southeast Asia. In July 1994, he wrote an article titled "The Strange Disappearance of Lance Cpl. James W. Jackson Jr." His story explained how "Sept 21, 1994, was the 25th anniversary of the day when Lance Cpl. Jackson walked into a Navy Hospital in Vietnam and vanished into thin air. Since that day in 1969 there has been absolutely no trace of Jackson nor any indication how or why he was swallowed up the moment he stepped through the doors of the 3rd Medical Battalion hospital in Quang Tri for treatment of a minor shrapnel wound."

Jackson had been wounded in the explosion that occurred during the abandonment of FSB Russell, shortly after the CH-53 evacuated my platoon. The explosion was blamed on the two former NVA scouts, who were believed to have ignited the daisy chain by dropping a cigarette into a pit containing explosives. Witnesses attested that Jackson was placed on the medevac at FSB Russell and arrived at the hospital in Quang Tri. Two corpsmen assisted Jackson as he walked in. That was the last time Jackson was ever seen alive, the last time his body was seen at all. He wasn't even missed for three weeks until his parents inquired about his location.

His mother, Rudeen West, is quoted in Martz's article as saying, "The Marine Corps lost my son. I had prepared myself for the possibility my son might die in Vietnam. I was ready for him to be wounded or captured or any of the things you expect in war because I was the mother of a Marine. But I wasn't ready for him to be lost without any explanation and that's what happened."

The Marine Corps must have been embarrassed about the incident. All accidents are regrettable, but this one resulted in two Marines being killed and 15 others wounded, and, in addition, Lance Cpl. Jackson could not be accounted for and was later declared dead. Part of the confusion resulted from the fact that two different Marines named Jackson were thought to have been medevac'd from FSB Russell that day. There was also the disappearance of the two Kit Carson scouts, who may have died if they hadn't escaped.

We soon had two new squads of Marines to replace the ones lost in the explosion, and a new CO. The initial confusion about Jackson may have intensified because our regiment was withdrawn to Okinawa six weeks after the disappearance, before the Marine Corps acknowledged and then investigated the incident. They eventually concluded that there really wasn't an explanation for Lance Cpl. Jackson's disappearance. He simply vanished, like the short-lived firebase named Russell.

The official Marine Corps Article 32 hearing testimony was the basis for Ron Martz's article on the strange disappearance of James W. Jackson Jr. In 2015, after writing these stories, I contacted Ron Martz so I could show him what I had written about FSB Russell. He advised me that he has changed his conclusions about Jackson's disappearance. Martz admitted to me that he has been obsessed by this incident since 1983, and in a recent e-mail said he "can't let it go." He reevaluated all of the considerable testimony taken by the Marine Corps on Jackson's disappearance, conducted new interviews, and prepared another detailed report titled, "Bringing Jimmy Home: The Case For GYSGT James W. Jackson, Jr."

This new report contains Martz's opinion that Jackson was not medevac'd to the hospital in Quang Tri from FSB Russell. He concludes that much of the testimony that was given regarding Jackson's evacuation was inaccurate and influenced by faulty memory and the confusion caused by the explosion. He believes that Jackson was buried in a collapsed bunker and never discovered, and no one wanted to admit that they may have left a Marine behind. Martz's conclusions are detailed here in Appendix A. He anticipates that an investigative team will return to Vietnam and search the FSB Russell hilltop, once again, to determine if any of Jackson's DNA or other remains can be found. The mystery surrounding Jimmy Jackson's sad fate is the incomplete final chapter of FSB Russell's story.

WELCOME HOME

In early October 1969, after six months leading 2nd Platoon, I was reassigned to our battalion's S-3 operations unit located in the rear area at Dong Ha. I began working for the same major with whom I had yelled at in frustration over the radio during the August sapper attack. No mention was ever made by him about that night's battle, and he bore no grudges with me for my impatient words. I enjoyed my time in operations and continued in that role after our regiment was withdrawn to Okinawa.

Before leaving Lima Company, I met with my platoon to say goodbye. It was an unemotional meeting; I wished them well and introduced them to their new platoon commander. Afterward, I spoke privately with Blitner and thanked him for his loyalty, advice, and support, and he expressed similar sentiments to me. After the farewell meeting, I boarded a helicopter to Dong Ha and soon found the bar constructed from tin and ammo-box lumber, where I enjoyed my first cold beer since I left Cua Viet in May.

Shortly after arriving at battalion headquarters, I left for my Rest & Recuperation (R&R) in Sydney, Australia,. All U.S. servicemen were allowed a one-week R&R to selected locations in nearby countries sometime during their tour, and I chose Sydney for my destination. After arriving in Australia and being greeted by an R&R planning committee, I decided to visit a sheep station in Queensland operated by Mr. and Mrs. Lamb (their real name), who generously welcomed American soldiers and Marines visiting on R&R. The deciding factor in choosing their ranch was the fact they had three daughters about my age. I imagined having stimulating conversations with these young women, but it turned out they had moved out of the house to live in Sydney.

It wasn't long after returning from R&R that our regiment was withdrawn to Okinawa. The shroud of anxiety that encompassed most of us lifted when our plane reached cruising altitude after leaving Da Nang. Not long after landing in Okinawa, I realized that this was going to be an enjoyable place to be stationed for the remaining six months of my tour.

We ordered our meals from menus at the officers' mess hall, our laundry was washed and our boots shined by someone else, and we were clean. The bars in Kin Village entertained us. If a young man's definition of pleasure was "wine, women, and song," Okinawa delivered. I spent the last six months of my tour in Okinawa and Mount Fuji, Japan, where we were sent for six weeks of cold-weather training. It was all agreeable, and the worries of combat were behind us. The contrast between the pleasures of Okinawa and the agony of Vietnam was profound. I suppose it was like a WWII veteran leaving the front for a weekend in Paris.

I also have stories about Okinawa and Japan. Like the time I pretended I knew jujitsu, making a few moves, to discourage the bouncers at a bar on Mount Fuji after we disputed the bill charges. They believed my act; we paid what we thought was the correct amount, walked out, and avoided a fight.

Then there was the story of "Butterfly," a pretty bar girl from Kin Village. Again, we were being stubborn by not leaving the bar when it closed, preferring to continue our conversation with Butterfly. But soon I heard a crash and felt the glass as a whisky bottle broke over my head. We ended up in an Okinawan jail before being picked up by the Marine military police (MPs) and transported back to base. The next morning we were ordered to explain our behavior to the battalion commander. The colonel went easy on us by just chewing us out.

Another time we rode horses into a bar. They were small horses that fit through the bar door, and we'd been riding them on the beach. Truth be told, I'm not sure I actually rode one into the bar; the memory is a blur and perhaps just wishful thinking. What can I say? We felt invincible after surviving Vietnam, especially after too many drinks. Sometimes we broke the rules and did exactly what we wanted, however stupid. You could say (if you were generous) that we were trying to regain the innocence of being boys again—I've never felt more alive. We knew that whatever punishment we received, they weren't going to send us back to war before our military commitment was over. My desire to continue helping in Vietnam was gone.

When I returned to the United States from Okinawa at the end of my 13-month tour, I landed at the nearly deserted Los Angeles Airport late at night and boarded the final flight back to my home in Columbia, Missouri. My family, of course, was glad I'd made it home alive, but the protests I soon witnessed at the University of Missouri campus gave me a truer indication that support for the war effort and appreciation for my Vietnam service had changed. Vietnam veterans didn't initially receive the same enthusiastic level of appreciation that other war veterans from WWII, Iraq, and Afghanistan have rightfully experienced. That was probably due to the controversy about the many failed goals envisioned for Vietnam. The protesters were passionately expressing the feeling that something was very wrong. Returning vets were the personification of U.S. failures.

I never thought I needed any help closing the Vietnam chapter in my life, but writing these stories brought back old memories, and a stranger's kind words convinced me I was mistaken. On a recent vacation to Williamsburg, Virginia, I approached an African American man about my age who was wearing a cap with "Vietnam Veteran" embossed above the brim. I asked where he'd served, and then told him where I'd been. After our brief conversation, I waved goodbye, and his parting words to me were, "Welcome home." It's been 46 years since Vietnam, and I've had strangers thank me for my service, but his choice of words warmed me and felt good to hear. He may have needed to hear the same sentiment; after all, he was the one wearing the Vietnam cap. If he ever reads this story, he should know that his words to a fellow Vietnam veteran were appreciated and won't be forgotten.

Since my conversation with the "Vietnam Veteran," I've done a lot of thinking on why his words "welcome home" were soothing to me and important to hear. I've decided that his words were more embracing and forgiving than simply thanking me for my service. For me, his words eased the guilt of participating in a failed war. It's true that joining the Marine Corps and going to

Vietnam was the right thing for me to do. I was supporting my country, and I'm proud of my service and military performance and view my experience positively. The U.S. government mounted a very impressive effort in Vietnam, and gave the South Vietnamese a good opportunity to form a successful and popular democratic government. Unfortunately, the South Vietnamese people did not adequately support Diem's administration or any of the successive governments of South Vietnam. Not enough of them sufficiently embraced our efforts, to win their "hearts and minds," to overcome the coalition that Ho Chi Minh represented. But with Vietnam there's plenty of guilt to go around. U.S. policy toward Vietnam was always flawed. Our citizens share responsibility for not paying enough attention before troops were committed in 1965.

As is always the case, the decisions that were made by our leaders led our country down the path we followed; like an ocean liner, it's never easy for a country to reverse course. The end result wasn't what we hoped for and brought a great amount of anguish to many Americans and Vietnamese. Regardless, there was honor in the effort and service of hundreds of thousands of my fellow citizens who served in the military. We listened to our country's leaders, gave up what we'd been doing, and offered our lives in support of our country's goals in Vietnam.

But offering support is not the same as winning wars. Nearly all U.S. troops were either drafted or had enlisted knowing they were likely to be drafted. They didn't want to be there and most lacked inspiration for anything but keeping themselves alive. This is not meant as a criticism, only an observation of a consequence of rational thinking. While our troops behaved courageously, they knew they needed only to survive a 12 or 13 month tour before going back to the "world." Their draft commitment was for only two years and when they returned from Vietnam they were often released early. The NVA and VC soldiers needed to survive the entire long war. Their troops had a seriousness that we couldn't equal. Their lives were routinely sacrificed by their leaders in ways our country would seldom attempt, because their ground troops represented the North Vietnamese government's only viable weapon. I'm thankful U.S. troops weren't often sacrificed in that way, but it reminds me of how difficult it is to win a war in foreign lands, when our own homeland is not at risk.

Ho Chi Minh began North Vietnam's fight against the French in 1945 and continued the fight against South Vietnam and the United States until he died from a heart attack in 1969. Ho's goals to free Vietnam from foreign influence were finally achieved in 1975, 30 years after they were begun, when the North Vietnamese took control of Saigon and South Vietnam.

While U.S. troops won most of the battles, we still lost the war. We had the resources to win if American and South Vietnamese support had been sustained or if we had invaded North Vietnam with ground troops to prevent war supplies from reaching South Vietnam. We feared that invading the North would have risked escalating what was a regional conflict into a much more dangerous war with Russia and China. We thought we could succeed by defending the South with our firebase and combat based war. But the North's increasing support and enduring will to control Vietnam's destiny was stronger than ours, and that made all the difference.

A LETTER TO MY CHILDREN ABOUT VIETNAM

It would have been better to have fought in a popular war—and a war that we'd won—but my war was Vietnam.

I lost two close friends in the war and have touched their names on the Vietnam Memorial Wall in Washington, D.C. Dale Jackson, a high school friend, and Phil Huth, a Basic School buddy, both died in 1969. During my six months with Lima Company, 3rd Battalion, 4th Marines, my company suffered 21 dead and at least 54 wounded. Over the years, it became apparent to me that our Vietnam policies were flawed, and our society continues to have a great amount of anger and misunderstanding about Vietnam. As an amateur historian, I became curious about the events that led to our country's participation. Why were we there? It's the question

I imagine you'd want to ask, and I want to be the one giving you the answer since there are so many divergent opinions about Vietnam. I'm proud of my service and loyalty during that time, but the question remains. Why did we do it?

Serving in Vietnam did not make me an expert on why we were there, but it motivated me to study and try to understand the experience. I've reread my old letters that my mother saved for me. I've reviewed "online information" about Khe Sanh, the Ho Chi Minh Trail, Hill 950, FSB Russell, sappers, and the location of villages and bases in Quang Tri Province. I've reread Ron Martz's story, "The Strange Disappearance of Lance Cpl. James W. Jackson Jr.," and his new report, "Bringing Jimmy Home." I've also reread Graham Greene's *The Quiet American*, and Andrew J. Basevich's analysis of Greene's book in *World Affairs* magazine. I've read Tim O'Brien's *The Things They Carried*, which inspired me to write these stories. I've studied The History Place website's presentation on the Vietnam War, which listed in chronological order the important events that occurred. I've read parts of Robert McNamara's book, *In Retrospect: The*

Tragedy and Lessons of Vietnam, David Halberstam's *The Best and the Brightest*, and John S. Bowman's *The Vietnam War: An Almanac.*

This research may not have made me an expert, but it has given me enough information to form opinions about our participation in Vietnam. I organized facts taken from The History Place presentation and McNamara's book, *In Retrospect*, into a synopsis detailed below. With all of this information in mind, and with the advantage of hindsight, I offer this analysis of "why we were there."

Following World War II, the victorious Allied Powers allowed France to retain control over Vietnam, one of their former colonies before the war. In 1945, Ho Chi Minh, taking exception to world authority and French colonialism, declared himself president of Vietnam and asked President Truman for U.S. recognition. His request was ignored. On December 19, 1946, Ho began what became known as the First Indochina War against the French. In 1950, Ho Chi Minh received recognition and support from Russia and China. In support of France, President Truman authorized the first U.S. military aid on July 26, 1950, one month after ordering U.S. ground troops to fight in Korea.

I can understand why we would support our WWII ally, France, against what the United States viewed as a communist attack against French colonial Indochina, but this military aid was the first small step leading to our war in Vietnam.

Dwight Eisenhower became president in 1953 and increased the amount of aid to France in support of their fight against North Vietnamese "communism." Eisenhower first expressed his "Domino Theory" in 1954, which speculated that a communist victory in Indochina would cause other surrounding countries to fall into communism like dominoes. A year before, in 1953, the Korean War had ended with the creation of North and South Korea. The United States continued to maintain a strong military presence in South Korea after the war ended. Today, South Korea is a dynamic democracy, and our military support remains in place.

Meanwhile in Vietnam, France was losing the Indochina War in 1954 and asked the United

States for substantially more aid, including ground troops. Their request was ultimately rejected, which indicates to me that the United States had "second thoughts" about French control and perhaps the concept of colonialism in general. France surrendered their airbase, Dien Bien Phu, as a result of the Viet Minh siege, on May 7, 1954. That was the final battle of the First Indochina War, and France withdrew in defeat, ending their colonialism in Vietnam. U.S. policy rejected French colonialism in Vietnam, but our fight to prevent Ho Chi Minh from expanding his control to include South Vietnam was only beginning.

Later in 1954, the Geneva Accords divided Vietnam, at the 17th parallel, creating South Vietnam, with General Ngo Dinh Diem in control, and North Vietnam, ruled by Ho Chi Minh. The Geneva Accords called for an election in 1956 to determine a leader to reunify the entire country. The United States later prevented that election, apparently because it feared Ho Chi Minh would prevail. The United States supported General Diem as president of South Vietnam and wouldn't risk loss of U.S. influence in the south by having a unifying election. U.S. policy toward Vietnam was similar to our policy in Korea, but it was carried out in a more secretive manner. In both cases the policy conceded the northern part of each country to the communists and retained the southern part as a U.S. ally. Eisenhower increased the level of support and later began to send advisors to train the South Vietnamese Army.

The novel, *The Quiet American*, written by Graham Greene in 1955, seemed accurate describing U.S. behavior toward Vietnam. The novel's "Quiet American" character, Alden Pyle, worked for the CIA (Central Intelligence Agency) and lived in Saigon during the final year of French control. He was naïve about Vietnam but forthright and earnest in his personal dealings. His CIA goal was to find a general that could unite and lead South Vietnam and accept U.S. influence and assistance. Pyle described the CIA plan as being the "third way." The "first way" could be interpreted as a "hands–off policy" toward South Vietnam, which would have led to a North Vietnamese victory. The "second way" could be described as continued military support for French colonialism in Vietnam.

After 1954, when the United States ended support for French colonialism and began supporting General Diem, it became increasingly apparent that President Diem was incapable of gaining the broad backing of his countrymen. Ho Chi Minh, however, became the charismatic leader of the north and also gained increasing influence in the south. In 1959, Ho declared an armed revolution to reunite the entire country and began the conflict against South Vietnam and its U.S. ally. Thus began the second Indochina war, the one Americans think of as the "Vietnam War," even though most Americans didn't know we were in it until 1965, when the Marines landed at Da Nang.

The United States made its first error in judgment during the Truman and Eisenhower administrations by not recognizing that Ho Chi Minh was capable and likely to unify and lead Vietnam. Our leaders must have calculated that we could defeat Ho's efforts in spite of his popularity by providing support, initially to France and then to the South Vietnamese. With perfect foresight, we might have recognized that Ho was primarily a nationalist and someone we could work with. If we had offered Ho some recognition or compromise when he requested it in 1945, perhaps we could have aligned his ideology toward capitalism instead of communism. We would have been abandoning our ally, France, but that's just what we ended up doing in 1954. We didn't do it to help Ho Chi Minh, but rather to begin our "third way" support of General Diem. Eisenhower may have suspected that accomplishing our goals would be difficult, but he seemed confident that the United States could overcome the challenges. After all, he had been the commanding general of U.S. forces at the end of World War II and must have thought he knew how to win wars.

When Eisenhower left office in 1960, Diem was still serving as South Vietnam's unpopular president. Eisenhower advised President Kennedy to expect an armed conflict against Ho Chi Minh, who had just begun his war to unify North and South Vietnam. By that time, in July 1959, two U.S. advisors in Vietnam had been killed. Kennedy appointed Robert McNamara to be his Secretary of Defense and increased the number of advisors serving in South Vietnam. Kennedy eventually sent 16,000 "special advisors," who were not explicitly charged with engaging in combat, but rather expected to advise the South Vietnamese ARVN forces and direct U.S. support.

In October 1962, Kennedy confronted the Soviets during the Cuban missile crisis. In January 1963, three American helicopter pilots were killed in Vietnam. On November 2, 1963, the United States (with CIA involvement) mysteriously supported a coup that killed unpopular South Vietnamese President Diem and his brother. The United States had permitted its chosen South Vietnamese leader to be killed and replaced by a new South Vietnamese administration. Kennedy was assassinated three weeks later in Dallas on November 22, 1963, and Lyndon Johnson became president.

During 1964, President Johnson endured five successive coups in the South Vietnamese government and couldn't find or retain the right leader. The United States had lost control of the situation. This was a crucial problem for U.S. policy, because the North was firmly unified around Ho Chi Minh. How could the United States overcome

Ho Chi Minh's domination of Vietnam if we couldn't establish a government that was capable of competing for the support of the South Vietnamese people? The answer was we couldn't, unless we could defeat Ho and then establish a sufficiently popular South Vietnamese government, like we did in Korea. Johnson's fundamental mistake was escalating the war in 1965 by inserting ground combat troops, incorrectly believing our country would have the ability and resolve necessary to defeat North Vietnam.

In defense of Johnson's decision, his action was the continuation of U.S. policy supported by the Truman, Eisenhower, and Kennedy administrations, which attempted to influence outcomes in Vietnam. Johnson's action fulfilled John Kennedy's promise made in his 1961 inaugural address: "Let every nation know, whether it wishes us well or ill, that we shall pay any price, bear any burden, meet any hardship, support any friend, oppose any foe to assure the survival and success of liberty." Kennedy's noble and elegant rhetoric proved to be an aspiration that was too difficult for the United States to achieve.

In August 1964, the "Gulf of Tonkin incident" occurred, where a North Vietnamese attack at sea became our excuse to escalate the war and begin bombing North Vietnam. At that time, 85 percent of American citizens supported the bombing. By the end of 1964, there were 23,000 advisors in Vietnam but 170,000 Viet Cong and NVA. Johnson won the presidential election and was inaugurated in January 1965. Two of his aides sent him a memo advising that the war was not succeeding and he should either withdraw or substantially increase U.S. commitment. Johnson chose to escalate the war effort. This was the beginning of the ground combat phase of the war, and the number of troops sent to Vietnam increased each year until peaking at 543,000 in 1969, during the Nixon administration. According to The History Place, a tally of the year-end U.S. commitment was as follows:

1965: 184,300 U.S. troops

1966: 389,000 U.S. troops, estimated cumulative dead 5,008

1967: 463,000 U.S. troops, estimated cumulative dead 16,000

1968: 495,000 U.S. troops, estimated cumulative dead 30,000

1969: 543,000 U.S. troops at peak, by year end 428,000, estimated cumulative dead 40,024

1970: 280,000 U.S. troops, estimated cumulative dead 46,202*

1971: 156,800 U.S. troops, estimated cumulative dead 48,606*

1972: 16,000 U.S. advisors, other U.S. troops withdrawn, estimated cumulative dead 49,404*

1973: All U.S. troops and advisors gone as of March 29, 1973, estimated cumulative dead 57,446**

---

* The cumulative dead estimate came from sources other than The History Place

** The official tally included additional deaths from previous years and has since been increased. These numbers do not include the deaths recorded for U.S. allies, South Vietnam, South Korea, Australia, Thailand, New Zealand, Philippines, and Taiwan. The Vietnamese government reported 1,100,000 NVA and Viet Cong deaths during the war.

1975: Last Americans leave Saigon on April 30, 1975, as the NVA storm the city and take control

In Robert S. McNamara's 1995 book *In Retrospect*, he wrote: "I believe we could and should have withdrawn from South Vietnam either in late 1963 amid the turmoil following Diem's assassination or in late 1964 or early 1965 in the face of increasing political and military weakness in South Vietnam." McNamara served as Secretary of Defense beginning in 1962 with the Kennedy administration, and then served President Johnson in that role through 1967. This statement apparently reflected McNamara's eventual opinion, but he did not offer it as a recommendation to President Johnson in 1964 or 1965, before Johnson escalated the war by sending ground forces to Vietnam. McNamara stated that on November 1, 1967, more than two years after the insertion of U.S. ground troops, he sent a memo to Johnson outlining his concerns in Vietnam. That memo led to McNamara's removal as Secretary of Defense and his selection as president of The World Bank. McNamara is quoted as saying, "I do not know to this day whether I quit or was fired. Maybe it was both."

McNamara also wrote that Dick Helms, the director of the CIA at that time, sent a secret memo to President Johnson. "Dick Helm's secret memo shows that, in the fall of 1967, the CIA's most senior analysts believed we could have withdrawn from Vietnam without any permanent damage to U.S. or Western security." It's unfortunate that the CIA hadn't previously offered that advice and that McNamara did not express his eventual conclusions before combat troops were inserted. In 1967, according to McNamara, President Johnson had many other advisors who did not agree with the McNamara and Helm analysis. Certainly, McNamara's eventual view, which may not yet have been formulated in 1965, would have been a minority opinion. If McNamara had expressed that opinion with conviction before 1965, he probably would have been fired and Johnson still would have inserted troops.

North Vietnam's Tet Offensive, which included many separate attacks on U.S. positions, occurred on January 31, 1968. The siege of Khe Sanh began a week earlier, on January 21, 1968, and lasted until July; it is considered by many to have been part of the Tet Offensive. While nearly all of the Offensive's many battles were won by the Americans, they were conclusive evidence of the North's determination. Most historians consider the Tet Offensive to be the turning point of the war. The widespread media coverage convinced the American public that the war could not be won.

President Johnson, feeling the weight of responsibility in Vietnam, announced on March 31, 1968, that he would not run or accept the upcoming nomination for president. This declaration, in my opinion, was Johnson's capitulating response to his recognition that he had made a serious mistake in 1965 by ordering ground troops to enter Vietnam. He probably realized that he'd lost the support of his countrymen and may have realized that public opinion in Vietnam was going against us as well. I believe that an increasing number of Vietnamese were beginning to think of us as they had the French colonialists and began to question our motives. Many must have thought that Ho was a devil, but at least he was "their" devil. Johnson must have concluded that he should turn the conduct of the war over to a different administration. He must have foreseen the political battles that awaited him if he continued in Vietnam without sufficient public support.

On January 20, 1969, Richard Nixon was inaugurated president. During the election he had promised to get the country out of Vietnam. Through April 1969, however, he increased U.S. troop levels and bombing in Vietnam. It appears that Nixon was feigning resolve in order to obtain the best deal possible for the United States at the peace talks in Geneva. In the summer of 1969, Nixon announced the beginning of the systematic withdrawal of troops, with the 3rd Marine Division and my unit being among the first to leave. The 3rd Marine Division's 3rd Battalion, 9th Marines had been the first to arrive in 1965 at Da Nang, hence the first to leave.

I now believe that during the time I led my infantry platoon in 1969, Nixon and a majority of U.S. political leaders had already come to the conclusion that the United States should withdraw from Vietnam. Withdrawing from a war, while paying lip service to winning, is a deception. If your leaders don't believe in the mission, it's bound to have negative consequences for the troops in the field. Rather than negotiating a hasty retreat at the peace talks in Geneva, our policy makers attempted to turn the conduct of the war over to the South Vietnamese ARVN troops and the government of South Vietnam (a policy known as Vietnamization.) The policy came with a promise that the United States would return if the South Vietnamese government required our aid. That assurance reminds me of similar promises made when we withdrew from Iraq (and Afghanistan).

Both Nixon and South Vietnamese government officials must have suspected that without U.S. troop support, South Vietnam would fall. Nixon's policy was deceiving and insincere, but he probably thought it was necessary to complete the abandonment that would soon follow. The Vietnamization policy resulted in four additional years of war and the loss of 27,446 more American lives. It betrayed the commitment our government made to our own troops and to the South Vietnamese and it failed to provide the United States with sufficient political cover for our abandonment. By April 30, 1975, when the ARVN forces were defeated and the U.S. Embassy in Saigon frantically abandoned, Nixon had resigned the presidency in disgrace as a result of Watergate. Gerald Ford was our new president, and he lacked the support and ownership in the war to muster a counteroffensive to rescue South Vietnam in 1975.

I suppose Nixon would say that Vietnamization gave the South Vietnamese a final chance to prevail. But it actually was more of a "face saving gesture," and the war's outcome was really determined when the United States began its troop withdrawal in 1969. After the withdrawal was initiated, I sensed that the United States was losing its resolve to win. I didn't appreciate the politics of the situation, but for me, I knew enough to avoid any unnecessary heroic action and to focus on getting my platoon home alive. I feel certain that my sentiments were shared by fellow Marines, peers, and commanders. While welcoming 3rd Marine Division's departure, we couldn't avoid thinking that our withdrawal would negatively affect the war's outcome.

The change in public opinion against the Vietnam War started after ground troops were inserted in 1965 but increased dramatically in 1968, following the Tet Offensive. Initially, after the August 1964 Gulf of Tonkin incident, which triggered the beginning of combat, 85 percent of U.S. citizens thought bombing North Vietnam was the correct course. In 1965, the public was unaware of the challenge that awaited us in Vietnam and expected a quick victory. Public support evaporated in 1968 when victory was delayed, just like it did after 2005 in Iraq and Afghanistan. Our citizens bear responsibility for this lack of resolve, but credit, I suppose, for finally getting the Vietnam policy right. It's too bad so many lives were wasted in the process.

North Vietnam's brand of communism engulfed the entire country after 1975. Many South Vietnamese officials escaped to the United States, were killed, or were sent to "reeducation camps." Meanwhile, in neighboring Cambodia, the Khmer Rouge, a radical communist organization, came to power in 1975. Khmer Rouge control resulted in the public extermination that came to be known as the "killing fields of Cambodia." That consequence fulfilled Eisenhower's prediction from his Domino Theory that a communist victory in Vietnam would result in other nearby governments falling like dominos into communism. An estimated two million Cambodian citizens, representing 25 percent of its population, were killed by their own government. That's almost twice the number of NVA and Viet Cong soldiers killed during the entire Vietnam War. Interestingly, in 1979 the Khmer Rouge government was removed from power by the North Vietnamese and replaced by a more moderate Cambodian communistic government. That was the destiny of Southeast Asia, and our participation in the Vietnam War may have only delayed the outcome.

As of 2015, the prevalence of worldwide communism has declined, and the United States has a tolerable, friendly relationship with Vietnam, in spite of the previous conflict. With hindsight, we can recognize that we shouldn't have inserted ground combat troops in 1965 without having a well-supported South Vietnamese government in place. That was the crucial error brought on by the well-intentioned policies of the Truman, Eisenhower, Kennedy, and Johnson administrations. And when U.S. public opinion turned against the war after 1968, Nixon should have brought the war to a speedier conclusion.

I returned to Columbia, Missouri, in 2015 to attend the 50th reunion of my high school class of 1965. I returned because my friend and Vietnam veteran, Gary Blackmore, had organized a memorial commemorating our four classmates, Larry Coleman, Dan Heibel, Steve Irvin and Dale Jackson, killed in Vietnam. All four served in infantry units, three Marine and one Army. Of those four, Dale Jackson was my closest friend.

Accompanied by motorcycle honor guards and many of my classmates, I drove the 70 miles to stand near his gravesite in a small town in northwest Missouri. Dale had asked his mother to bury him, if he was killed in Vietnam, in that distant family plot next to his uncle. He didn't want his mother wasting her time visiting him every day like he knew she would if he was buried in Columbia. The simple headstone had darkened from the algae

Dale Jackson's grave
(photo by Gary Blackmore)

that had grown there. It looked like it had been placed there a long time ago, and indeed, it's been 46 years. I couldn't help but be reminded of the life I've enjoyed after Vietnam that Dale wasn't able to experience. As most Americans now realize, it is past time for the anger, blame, and resentment about Vietnam to end; we should concentrate instead on the sacrifices that were willingly made by those who participated in the war and, especially, those who were killed.

Knowing the history of our relationship with Vietnam since 1945 has helped me to understand why the decisions were made that led us to fight in Vietnam and why many of those decisions were mistakes. I can appreciate the reasons for the war protests and only wish that our country's reflection had occurred before ground troops were inserted in 1965, but most citizens were unaware at that time. The knowledge gained from my research has helped me find closure for my part in the Vietnam experience. For our country, I worry that public opinion is not always well reasoned and sometimes uninformed, and the betrayal of promises has consequences.

We paid a high price in lives, resources, and credibility for our Vietnam mistakes. Our leaders will continue to make mistakes, as all humans do, but I hope their judgment, at least, is sincere. As for my own participation, at least I can say that when my country called, I tried to help.

ACKNOWLEDGEMENTS

Of all the characters described in these stories, Fortney and Mobot are the only two that are composites rather than individual Marines from my company. I fictionalized their participation in one of the LP teams killed at the hilltop where sappers overran 3rd Platoon. Marines in both LP teams were indeed killed, but I have no memory that any of the composite Marines representing either Fortney or Mobot were among them.

I want to thank my wife, Brenda, for encouraging me to write these stories and for her helpful comments that made the stories better. I also received encouragement and suggestions from my son Brian and daughter Whitney, sisters Carol and De and brother Len, brothers-in-law Jim and John, sister-in-law Linda, and daughter-in-law Blair. Many old friends also gave me support. Ron Martz was very generous in sharing information about Jimmy Jackson and FSB Russell. Ann Seifert provided excellent editing and useful suggestions.

My father died in 2013 before I began writing my stories, but his service in WWII and the way he lived his life has always inspired me. I'm also very grateful that my mother saved the letters I sent home, and I thank her for the tears she tried to conceal when I boarded the plane taking me to Vietnam.

APPENDIX A

From "Bringing Jimmy Home" by Ron Martz

Conclusions and Opinions

(1) The conclusion made by the Article 32 board that Jackson walked into the hospital and disappeared is illogical and unreasonable.

(2) No thorough search for remains was made on FSB Russell either the day of the explosion or by search parties subsequently sent back.

(3) Members of the search party did not know that anyone, other than the two Vietnamese scouts, was missing. Thus, when they were told that the scouts were left on the hill, they were predisposed to believe that any remains they found would be of the scouts.

(4) More than one set of human remains was seen on the hill and left behind because of the assumption that they were those of the scouts.

(5) Neither MAJ Seeburger, who made the final decision, nor 1LT Ogilvie, who viewed the remains, was qualified to make an assessment of the size, ethnicity, or any other identifying characteristics of any remains. Since neither knew Jackson was missing, it can only be surmised that had they known that, a more substantial effort would have been made to recover and identify those remains.

(6) Even after it was discovered that Jackson was missing, no effort was made to recover and identify the remains.

(7) Jackson most likely was left on the hill due to the confusion and chaos after the accidental explosions.

(8) Desmond testified (p. 46) that "There was just too much commotion. Everybody was shaken up." He also said (p. 47) that he was

"dizzy from the smoke and the clothes that were burning on the scout." How much did that affect his judgment and what he saw? And how much did the flash burns he suffered to his eyes affect what he saw?

(9) Gray testified: "There was quite a bit of confusion" after the explosion, but was adamant in a 1985 interview that Jackson was on the helicopter.

(10) Nesbitt, the first platoon's right guide said (p. 106), "there was so much fire and confusion."

(11) Wiltse was wounded in the explosion (p. 41), but was not medevaced until the following day. He was gone about two days, so there is a lapse in command and control and accountability for James Jackson. Also, was Wiltse suffering from fatigue and/or shock as a result of the explosion, fire, confusion, and mass casualties of the day so that he thought he saw Jackson, but actually saw another Marine?

(12) The stress and confusion of that day on FSB Russell may, in the reconstruction of events weeks later, have convinced the key eyewitnesses that they put him on the helicopter. As the Navy psychiatrist testified (p. 121), Jackson "becomes the real person because everybody is talking about him and that, therefore, he must have been Jackson."

(13) Wood, the battalion commander, testified (p. 59) that he had become convinced based on the eyewitness testimonies of Gray, Steve Jackson, Desmond, and Wiltse that "I was able, initially, to get Lance Corporal JACKSON off the hill." He seems to have dismissed the possibility that there was a case of mistaken identity and that Jackson might have been left on the hill. He based his assumption that Jackson had gotten off the hill on what appears to be suspect eyewitness accounts.

(14) Gray also dismissed the possibility that it was a case of mistaken identity. But it was Gray who initially was asked by Wiltse whether he

knew what happened to Jackson, indicating that neither of them initially was sure of their identification. And Steve Jackson may have been influenced by Gray, who came to him asking if that was James Jackson on the helicopter.

(15) Murray said in a 1984 interview that although he was struck by the "unaltered recollection" of Gray and Wiltse "that they actually personally recalled putting him on the helicopter," that over the years he has had a problem reconciling their certainty with Jackson's disappearance. "I guess I have come to the opinion over a period of time that in the heat of battle . . . that in the confusion that resulted after the explosion . . . as more plausible that we left him there, than that we didn't leave him there."

(16) But the idea that Jackson walked into triage and simply disappeared defies all logic and reason. The only logical and most reasonable explanation is that he was left on the hill as a result of the confusion and chaos.

(17) Although the information offered in these pages is not indisputable proof that Jackson's remains are still on that hill, we believe that the preponderance of evidence in this case is such that it is sufficient to justify an excavation of FSB Russell in search of the remains of GYSGT James W. Jackson, Jr.

Leaving his college deferment behind, this son of a WWII veteran enlisted in the Marine Corps in 1967, to help in the Vietnam fight. He was assigned to Officer Candidate School, became a 2nd Lieutenant and led a platoon in combat in 1969, when he was only 21. As the war progressed, the country's enthusiasm and support deteriorated and upon his return to the U.S., the author discovered that his service wasn't always respected as being patriotic and worthwhile. Over the years his interest in history prompted him to try to explain why. *The Sun Sets On Vietnam* describes his combat experience in a very personal way, and includes his own photos and watercolor illustrations. His reflections on the war have helped him resolve the experience.

After Vietnam, the author returned home and left the Marine Corps in 1971. He completed his business degree at the University of Missouri and began a 40 year career, serving first as a trust officer and then a financial advisor. He retired in 2013 and lives with his wife in Helena, Montana.